If the World Fits, You're the Wrong Size

The Christian in a Non-Christian World

Bill Stearns

This book is designed for your personal reading pleasure and profit. It is also designed for group study. A leader's guide, with visual aids (SonPower Multiuse Transparency Masters) and Rip-Offs (student activity booklets) are available from your local Christian bookstore or from the publisher.

VICTOR BOOKS

a division of SP Publications, Inc.
WHEATON, ILLINOIS 60187

Offices also in Fullerton, California • Whitby, Ontario, Canada • Amersham-on-the-Hill, Bucks, England

Library of Congress Catalog Card Number: 81-51425
ISBN: 0-88207-588-8

© 1981, SP Publications, Inc. All rights reserved
Printed in the United States of America

VICTOR BOOKS
A division of SP Publications, Inc.
Box 1825 • Wheaton, Ill. • 60187

This one's for Ami

What You'll Be Reading

Author's Note

I remember it clearly. The British-accented camp speaker was rolling his r's as he talked about the dazzling *Chrrrristian* life. I sat there with my sunburned nose peeling in flakes, a fever blister forming just above my lip. My jeans had shrunk, so they slid up above my sock tops when I sat down. Just before camp my dad had performed one of his famous kamikaze attacks on my hair with his Save-Money-By-Cutting-Your-Kids'-Hair-At-Home clippers. And some clod had walked off with my deodorant.

"Now," the speaker asked, "how many of you Christians feel as if you've chosen a dull lifestyle? Uh-uh, I don't want you to raise your hands on this. Just think about it. Do you feel like an underdog in life because you're a Christian? Don't raise your hands. . . ."

I raised my hand.

Christianity *was* pretty dull to me. I always seemed to feel out of place. All the excitement, challenge, color, and pizzazz seemed to be on the other side of the fence—in the world. It seemed as if I were on the naive/passive/wouldn't-harm-a-flea side, and over the fence were the sophisticated/adventurous/tough worldly people. Then . . .

One day I discovered the truth: There is no fence. The world is over here too. That was news to panic by, since I had to admit I was scared to death of the real world.

It was an uphill climb to begin living real Christianity in the real world. I had to realize that a lot of my energy had gone into conforming my lifestyle to traditional, *cultural* Christianity instead of to Christ. I had to be convinced that Jesus did not say, "Come unto Me, all ye that are weary and heavy-laden, and I will make you all the same."

I had to realize that in Christ I'm a strong man running a tough marathon (1 Corinthians 9:24). I'm a nothin's-going-to-stop-me boxer stepping into the ring (1 Corinthians 9:26-27). Now I'm finding challenges, miracles. I'm discovering a Christian lifestyle that's unique to me.

Biblical Christianity *is* dazzling. Exhilarating. Incredible. Sometimes it's hard. But not dull. Never dull.

* * * *

Incidentally, this isn't one of those *How to Live the Proper Christian Lifestyle* books. I won't try to tell you how you should vote, what colors your clothes should be, or what kind of toothpaste you should use. It's more of a *primer* on how real Christianity involves every area of the whole person. (Spiritual truths are not just for spirits.) So don't expect one-size-fits-all answers. And don't expect all of life to be thoroughly examined. OK?

By the way, if you'd been sitting at that camp meeting, would you have felt that the Christian lifestyle was dull? Well, put your hand down. You *can* catch the risky idea of living real Christianity in the real world. And I want to help. So if some of this doesn't make sense, or if you belong to a youth group that could use some in-person motivation toward real Christianity in the real world, be sure to write. (Bill Stearns, Prairie Grove, Arkansas, U.S.A. 72753) I keep a crazy schedule, but I'll consider you a top priority. After all, we *are* in this together. . . .

Jesus said, "I am no more in the world; and yet they themselves are in the world. . . . They are not of the world, even as I am not of the world."
John 17:11, 14

I
THE DISCIPLE AND THE WORLD

1
Discipleship, the Real Stuff

Sticky salt air—even at three in the morning you could feel and taste it. The moon bounced across thick Gulf swells as our crew boat blasted away from Port Sulphur. Most of the roughneck crew had turned up for our hitch aboard an offshore oil rig. Slim was drunk; we'd had to throw him below into the cabin. He kept mumbling, "She goin' leave me this time. She ain't goin' be home." Tex and

Johnny started spitting tobacco juice on him through an open hatch.

"Got him that time, yep." Johnny's silver tooth gleamed in the moonlight. The boat roared on with a menace.

I flopped onto a pile of shrimp nets to squeeze some sleep from the hours it would take us to reach the rig. Maurice was pacing across the sweaty deck, shouting sailors' oaths to impress the new hand. I covered my ears with a life jacket.

"You ain't goin' to sleep anyhow." Maurice kicked me with a pointed cowboy boot. "Get up and listen to this."

"Drop dead," I said.

In an imitation Chicano accent, Maurice launched into his comedy routine about how an oil rig was a doper's dream. The new hand's eyes glistened and he laughed till he choked.

Maurice strutted. "Listen, worm—"

"Name's Jones," said the new man.

"Listen, worm. You get out there and the rig boss is called a tool *pusher*; so you got your own live-in pusher! Get it? And the joints: Y'know, the pipe sections are called *joints*. On our rig, man, you got joints 30 feet long! And every time you join those pipes you make a *connection*, man! And whenever the pipe's going in or out of the hole you take a *trip*, man. And—"

"Yeah, yeah." Jones grinned.

"And you know the lubricant stuff between the joints? Well, there's buckets and buckets of it. And it's called—yeah, you guessed it—*dope*! Dope in your hair, dope up your nose!"

"Yeah, I'm into dope," said Jones.

Maurice clamped a hand over Jones' mouth. "Hey, man. That's just joke-stuff." Maurice looked around the deck at the rest of the crew as they took turns spitting and looked off over the Gulf. "They'll kick you over to the barracudas, man. Don't say nothin' about really dopin' it. Huh, worm?"

The Formula

Jones turned out to be a bona fide dope fiend. But he was no worm. He knew how to handle himself on a rig. Just a few days into the hitch, I began to admire his skill as a roughneck. "You've been around rigs some, huh?" I asked him one day.

"Yeah. I owe it all to dope—and Jesus."

Just then the driller screamed some unintelligible orders. I determined to talk to Jones as soon as I got a chance. I thought it was a pretty intriguing formula: Jesus plus dope equals a top-notch roughneck.

I got my chance to talk to Jones one night after we'd lowered the derrick, while we were waiting for the tugs to show up to move the rig. We sprawled among the braces of the derrick, listening to a radio station from Mexico.

"Christianity's a farce," said Jones. "My dad was a preacher, so I know all about it. Our church was going to get a new piano. So when it gets there, everybody starts arguing about which side of the auditorium to put it on. So they start hassling my dad from both sides—threatening notes, phone calls at all hours—till finally he has a heart attack. We left those church people to decide for themselves where to put their piano."

"Which side did they choose?" asked Maurice.

Jones ignored the question. "Church people— they've got to meet at 11 o'clock Sunday mornings and every Sunday night like it's a sacred schedule."

"The boy sounds bitter," I said.

"Well, I am!" Jones nearly slipped off his brace. "I'm sick of it! You got to walk this particular aisle or God won't have you. You got to wear spiffy duds to God's house. That's what they think, anyway. God's house is people, not buildings. Call their preachers Reverends—'Reverend So and So.' The Bible never says nothin' 'bout calling anybody 'Reverend.' The word means 'terrible,' and the Bible only uses it for God Himself."

"You're a regular Bible scholar, huh?" I broke in. "But what you're talking about is cultural Christianity—Churchianity."

"It's all the same. If it really worked, there wouldn't be so much tacky stuff done in the name of Christ. Like I heard some righteous group in San Francisco wants to execute all the homos. That's *real* godliness."

"You're missing it again," I challenged. "That's not really Christianity."

"I say it is."

"OK. So what's your alternative?"

Jones leaned back and drew on his cigarette. "Dope," he finally answered. "Yeah, there's Somebody up there." He pointed to the bright canopy of stars over the Gulf. "But I don't worry about Him when I'm high."

The Grand Alternative

Then Jones began the tale of his grand alternative to Christianity: "I tossed my *I Ching* and I knew I was in for good stuff. Met this girl in Thibadeaux and married her the same night. We got stoned and the next thing I know I wake up and I'm bashing her head against the wall. Nearly killed her, I guess. So the next time I come off a hitch offshore, she's gone home to Mama."

"How long ago was this?" asked Maurice.

"About two years," said Jones. "So I go to her folks' house and try to see her and they lock the doors on me. Can you believe it? Nothing I can do, so I go downtown and get drunk and go back to the house about midnight and bash the back door in. Then I kind of blacked out. . . ." He paused to smoke again and we watched phosphorescent jellyfish drift under the rig.

"They tell me I grabbed Jill's mother," Jones continued. "Jill's my wife. Or she was. I kind of threw her around. Then her old man came running down the stairs with a shotgun, and I tried to kill him. So about then the cops show up and it takes four of 'em to take me. I woke up in the vet hospital over in Alabama about a week later. Little padded cells, funny men. So I got out of there in six months and went to New Orleans. Got picked up by a couple of transvestites. I was so high I didn't know what was happening. They stole everything I had and I couldn't get the cops to even look into it."

Maurice and I looked at each other.

"Then I kind of got into dealin'. We had this

party at my brother's house. I made up some homemade ice cream with shrooms and—"

"Shrooms?" I asked.

"Mushrooms, Stearns," explained Maurice. "You know? The kind that makes you feel funny?" He shrugged. "Forget it."

Jones was talking to himself more than to us now. "There was this girl my brother used to know in church and she didn't know about the ice cream and she, uh, she took a lot of it. Then she tried to drive home and got scared when she started trippin'." He stopped as if to listen to a song on the radio.

"What happened to the girl?" asked Maurice.

"She ran over two old ladies and a kid. They put her in the funny farm—for the rest of her life. Made an example of her to teach kids not to mess with dope. So, I been working offshore ever since.

"Got run off the last rig, though. They found my stash. I had it in an old deodorant tube but they brought dogs on the rig to sniff it out. I knew they were going to run me off so I got stoned. They dumped me off the crew boat just before we got to the dock. Guess they thought it was funny. I nearly drowned.

"So there I am, in the middle of the night. So I hit the bar just a ways down the peninsula. So I wake up in the parking lot still soaked—no bread, no place to go. That was two weeks ago. Once you guys' outfit finds out, they'll run me off too. Blackballed, right?"

"Life in the fast lane," I muttered. "Yeah, they're tight on dope here. Definitely." We listened to a couple of songs. Then I said, "And you call that an alternative, huh?"

"I'm not sure," Jones answered.

"How about a real alternative?"

"Religious?"

"No."

"Let's hear it."

The Real Thing

Jones' words buzzed in me like a coded alarm. I figured the Holy Spirit was making His move. So I began, "If any man come after Me—"

Jones swore and started to climb down.

I grabbed him by the hair. "Look, Jocko. I listened to yours. You *will* listen to mine." I slowly grinned. "OK?"

"Nothin' else to do," he said. He climbed back up and settled into a perch on the braces.

"Let's see," I said. "If anybody will go after Christ, he's got to deny himself, take up his cross daily, and follow Him."[1]

"Oh, come on," Maurice groaned.

"Just shut up and listen." I kicked him with my steel-toed boot. It hadn't taken me long to figure out that in the oil patch, you don't reach roughnecks with sweet talk.

I continued, "You get sick of the fake Christianity and so do I. But where there's a counterfeit, there's the real thing, OK? So here it is in one fat nutshell, the real thing. Imagine this horizontal line, like the horizon on the Gulf. Above the line is God and Life and good stuff. But below the line is me. I'm not perfect like God so I can't be into His life—*the* Life. No matter how hard I try, I can never get perfect.[2] So God says that if I want to get into His Life I've got to first realize I can't do it on my own. I've got to quit trying to make it in my own strength. OK so far?"

Maurice yawned. "I liked Jones' story better."

"No, I'm with you," said Jones. "You're talkin' about the old nature."

"Yeah," I said, surprised. "OK. So imagine that I'm stuck in like a half-circle below the line. If I say to myself and God that I can make it on my own, I'm saying yes to my old imperfect nature. But if I *deny* my old self, then I can turn to God's way of getting me in on His Life."

"I know this stuff," said Jones. "Now how about the cross bit?"

"Hold on. The way I say no to my old way of life and say yes to God is first to ask Him into my life.[3] Am I comin' through?"

"I know the story," said Jones. "God, as Jesus Christ, died and rose—"[4]

"So when I ask Him to be the boss of my life,[5] He comes inside me and brings His Life.[6] It's like completing the circle with Him included *in* me. He makes me a brand-new person inside. Then the cross thing—"

Maurice laughed. "I know about crosses to bear, man. You ought to see my mother-in-law."

Jones was intent. "I never understood that part. What about the cross?"

Maurice spit over the side.

"The cross means death to the old self, and new life in the new self.[8] It means daily saying no to the old me and saying yes to God's Life."[9]

"Pick up the cross and follow Me?" said Jones.

"Yeah," I said. "But not just follow.[10] I had a chicken named Ferdinand once. He thought he was a human being. He'd walk beside me like my good buddy. He even tried to play the piano, started doing all kinds of things more like a person than a chicken. I couldn't figure it out till I ran across the idea of *imprinting*. That means that an animal will take on the characteristics of whatever it's exposed to the most. That chicken was actually gettin' to be like me."

"Cluck, cluck-cluck," said Maurice.

"You're talkin' about becoming like Christ, right?"[11] said Jones. "Whoever you follow, you become like?"

"You know all this, don't you?"

"Yeah, yeah," he said. "It's just so easy to gloss over the basics in all the games that pass for Christianity."

"That's why I like to call the real thing *discipleship*. It's a good label for that basic pattern of denying the old self, living in the new self daily, and following in the steps of Christ to become more like Him. I'm not talkin' about cultural Christianity that's about nine-tenths artificial. That's more tradition than real life."

"I like that," said Jones, " 'cultural Christianity.' "

"I don't," I said.

"No, I mean the idea of separating the fakey stuff, the cultural Christianity, from the real thing, discipleship."

The Real World

"I'm getting sick," yawned Maurice. "You guys are like a couple of old hens. I used to go to a parochial school, and they cackled this stuff all day long. The whole trick, to me, is whether your 'real Christian discipleship' bit works in the mad, mad world—like it is, you know? I say it doesn't. That's why everybody turns to the fake version. It's nice and respectable."

"Hah!" I kicked Maurice again. "You've been listening, you toad!"

Jones nodded. "Real discipleship-type Christianity, in the real world."

"You got quite a background in Christianity, huh? Who would have thought?" I really was amazed as I wondered about Jones' relationship with Christ, and about wild Maurice's.

"Yeah," Jones mumbled. "My old man knew what he was talkin' about. Discipleship in the world."

"*In*," Maurice tried to sound like Billy Graham. "But not *of* the world!" and he turned up the radio.

I couldn't believe it; the seamiest turkeys in the oil field talking about Christian discipleship. I lay back against the braces and nodded up at the stars. *Thanks, Lord. It's been weird. But thanks. Guess You're putting just that much more pressure on me to live it, huh? To be a real disciple*—Suddenly the driller spotted us and started swearing and screaming up orders for busywork—*a real disciple in a very real world.*

---

[1]*Luke 9:23*
[2]*Romans 3:23*
[3]*John 1:12*
[4]*Romans 5:8*
[5]*Romans 10:9*
[6]*1 John 5:12*

[7]*2 Corinthians 5:17*
[8]*Romans 6:6-8*
[9]*Ephesians 4:22-24*
[10]*1 Peter 2:21*
[11]*Romans 8:29*

2
The Invisible System

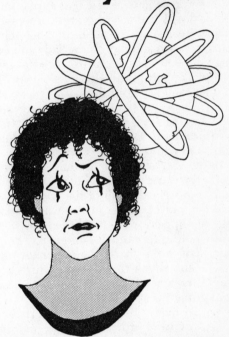

"A man of the world . . ." Henry started out on one of his lectures as we began a break. I was working the graveyard shift in a California warehouse, and Henry had decided I needed some instruction in the ways of the world. "Are you listenin', boy?"

"Yes sir, Henry," I replied. Henry, at 6'6", was a combination of football's Mean Joe Green and singer Jim Croce's Bad LeRoy Brown. In fact, Croce's lyrics could have been written about Henry instead of LeRoy: "All the women called him 'Treetop Lover,' all the men just called him 'Sir.'"

"A man of the world takes every opportunity," Henry preached, "even if it turns out bad. The other day, I was in this barbershop and I tell the man, 'Real sharp razor, huh? Nice, close shave.' So I sit down and there's this lady and I say, 'Come manicure my nails, darlin',' So we get to talkin' while I'm gettin' the shave and I say, 'How 'bout dinner tonight?' And she says, 'Oh, no.' 'Why not?' I say.

"'I'm married,' she says and shows me the ring. 'No problem,' I say. 'Just call your husband and tell the wimpy jerk you're workin' late.' 'The wimpy jerk,' she says, 'is shaving your neck.'"

Henry burst into laughter. "Man of the world, huh, boy? A real man of the world."

A couple of years later I was working with a hay-hauling crew out of a little town in Oklahoma. We would quit work at sundown. Then for entertainment we'd sit on the porch of our rooming house and watch the cars and trucks roll by. One day after work I was overjoyed to see a big-top tent going up at the edge of town.

"A carnival!" I jumped up and down.

"A revival," frowned Doug, my hay-hauling associate.

It was, in fact, a revival: tight-packed, sweating babies, women, boys, and grandfathers singing in the hot Oklahoma evening. When the singing ended a steely-eyed old preacher jumped up on the platform. I'll never forget what he said: "You want to be a highfalutin man of the world? Want to have the world by the tail? Live at the top of the world? Well, listen!" he leaped and thundered at Doug and me.

We listened.

"The world," he whispered loud enough to be heard at the other end of town, "the world . . . is flat! Flat! Like them pizzas. Yep, it looks juicy, invitin', enticin'. It tastes delicious—for a while. Then after you eat more and more and more, it gets cold and greasy and dull and nauseatin'." I knew what he meant. I once tried to eat two giant pepperoni pizzas. So I thought it was a good comparison: The world is flat like a pizza.

"No!" the preacher shouted at us again. "No, the world . . . the world is . . . square! Them in its clutches thinks us non-worldly folks are the square ones. But it's the world. It's the *world* that's square!"

I started nodding at his wisdom when the preacher roared again. "No! Listen, people!"

We listened.

"The world . . ." He drew out the words. "The world ain't in no shape at all."

What in the World?

What *is* this "world" that preachers and parents are always warning about? What does it really mean to be a man or woman of the world, to be worldly? Once I spoke at a retreat where a girl complained, "I really don't know what it's all about, but my mother just pleads with me to stay away from—" she rolled her eyes and drawled—"*worldliness*. It sounds so . . . so dramatic."

Christian parents sometimes do get melodramatic in their warnings about the world. That's because through the years they've caught on to something: The world can be dangerous. Deceptively dangerous. It can look like Las Vegas at night and turn into the Mojave Desert by morning. But let's try to cut through the illusion. Here's your big chance to see the world.

There are several words in the original Greek New Testament that are translated into English as "world." One Greek word, *kosmos*, is the "world" we're talking about. In the Greek, *kosmos* meant "that which is ordered, regulated." From *kosmos* comes our English word *cosmos* which refers to the well-ordered universe.

The Greeks used *kosmos* in several ways, but our focus is on the meaning of *kosmos* in Bible verses such as 1 John 5:19: "And the whole world lies in the power of the evil one." The "world" that we're to be *in* but not *of* has something to do with being ordered, regulated, and manipulated by the evil one, Satan.

"The World": Manipulated by Satan . . .

We can pick up two more tidbits on the "world" in Ephesians 6:12: "Our struggle is not against flesh and blood, but against the rulers, against the powers, against the world forces of this darkness, against the spiritual forces of wickedness in the heavenly places."

First, the verse points out that Satan has his group well *organized*. He's kingpin of the ultimate mob syndicate: He rules his turf through a team of lesser rulers, powers, and forces. He's got a racket going, a system. And he's "the godfather," the "god of this world" (2 Corinthians 4:4). The "world" is a Satan-regulated system.

Also notice that Satan's system is definitely low-profile. In fact, the rulers and powers and world forces operate in "darkness," in "heavenly places," in the spiritual dimension. The "world" is invisible!

I was a platoon guide in army boot camp. "Platoon guide" is a fancy name for a trainee who has to pass on the drill sergeant's orders to other trainees. He's an acting sergeant, without the authority of a sergeant. So I had lots of responsibility with no authority. If a soldier didn't want to follow my command, technically he didn't have to. Most of the guys knew what a pickle I was in, so they went along with me. Ralph didn't.

He looked just like the rest of us onionheads, but Ralph always stuck out—he wouldn't "fall in" when I yelled the command. I'd yell, "Hustle!" on a competitive forced march and Ralph would loll behind, picking his nose. He always pulled down our platoon scores.

After a month, I complained to the drill sergeant, "I quit. That's it. I can't get that picker to do anything with the rest of us."

"Time for the Boiler Room Treatment," the sergeant said grinning, "the BRT. I can't touch the kid, but maybe you can teach him a lesson. Understand?"

Now, it was not wise nor loving nor Christlike of me. But I decided I'd teach Ralphie a lesson with the BRT. I outweighed him by 20 pounds, so the BRT sounded like a quick solution to my problem.

That night Ralph and I stepped into the boiler room underneath the barracks. I casually clicked on the light and closed the door to the group of soldiers outside. Then I proceeded to pick a fight. I remember saying something clever like, "I've had enough of you, pudface," and shoving Ralph toward the wall. A few more shoves, and I readied a right cross to Ralph's head.

I began to step forward with my right foot, throwing my weight forward. I figured one good punch would do it. Suddenly Ralph leaped in the air, screamed, and kicked me in the teeth. I came to against the boiler wall. Ralph was smiling. I could hear the guys outside going, "Hey, Stearns really clonked Ralph with that one!"

I stood up, wondering if Ralph had just been watching too many kung fu movies. Then Ralph turned out the boiler room light. I never saw what happened next, but I certainly felt it!

For weeks afterward I had dreams of knifelike jabs hitting me from all sides, of smashing face-first into the wall, of groping for the door yelling, "Mama!"

Now, fighting is dumb. I was dumb to pick a fight. But that's not the point. What I experienced in that boiler room was the pain of fighting against somebody who was a better fighter. Somebody who—in the dark—I couldn't see. Needless to say, I made friends as soon as I could with good old Ralph.

Now put yourself in my place back then, and let's make the situation worse. Let's say Ralph is really out to get you. He wants to waste your body, to mess up your mind, to destroy every part of you. And let's say he's *always* invisible to you. And he's got a whole gang of terrorists that he sends after you. And you can't see them either.

Get it? Believe it or not, that's your situation. Only, your enemy isn't named Ralph. Your enemy is named Satan, which literally means "the adversary."

Think about it, and let's set out the findings of our "world" study so far:

"The World": Manipulated by Satan through an Invisible System . . .

Now, what does Satan regulate? What's in the world?

"All that is in the world, the lust of the flesh and the lust of the eyes and the boastful pride of life, is not from the Father, but is from the world" (1 John 2:16).

What makes up the world?

• **The lust of the flesh.** There's nothing wrong with desire. And there's certainly nothing wrong with the body, which "the flesh" means in this usage. But remember, the strong physical desires of the body—desires for food, for drink, for rest, for sexual pleasure—are prime targets for manipulation by the Enemy. Manipulated by Satan, natural desire becomes sinful, out-of-control *lust*.

• **The lust of the eyes.** Seeing something and wanting it strictly for your *ego's* sake is the second factor in worldliness. "The lust of the eyes" might include wanting to have just the right clothes, to look sophisticated by smoking cigarettes, to seem tough by swearing a lot, or to drive a car that people notice. The ego, then, is the second target area Satan tries to control.

• **The boastful pride of life.** "I did it *my* way," says a popular song by that title. The song basically promotes the idea of complete independence from man or God. It could be a theme song for this third area of worldliness, "the boastful pride of life."

God has given man a *free will*, so he can choose to do his own thing or follow God. Satan loves to get a person to decide to call all the shots by himself, to be his own god.

The enemy, Mr. Satan, wants to control all of you—every single part. And he's out to do it by appealing to your physical desires, your ego, and to your urge to call your own shots—to be your own god.

Remember the Garden of Eden scam? Genesis 3 not only shows how the Enemy ripped off Adam and Eve. It also outlines Satan's three-part plan for controlling mankind:

Part 1: Appeal to *the lusts of the flesh*. The strong desires of the body gave Satan the perfect setup to tempt Eve. At first Eve resisted by recounting God's commandment: "You shall not eat from it [the tree] or touch it, lest you die" (3:3). But then "The woman saw that the tree was good for food" (3:6). Satan used the classic world-system appeal to Eve's physical desires. He made his pitch right to her taste buds. And Eve swallowed the bait.

Part 2: Appeal to *the lust of the eyes*. "When

the woman *saw* that the tree was good for food, and that it was a delight to the *eyes*, and that the tree was desirable to make one *wise*, she took . . . and ate" (3:6, italics mine). When Eve saw the fruit, she wanted it because she believed Satan's line: "In the day you eat from it your eyes will be opened" (3:5). The old serpent hissed, "Grow up, Eve. Don't be naive. Broaden your horizons. What are you—old-fashioned?" So Satan manipulated Eve's ego.

Part 3: Appeal to *the boastful pride of life*. Satan promised the ultimate to Eve: "God knows that in the day you eat from it your eyes will be opened, and you will be like God" (3:5). Satan hit her with all three barrels. And his third shot came in the form of a message: "Forget what God says about Himself. You can do a better job! I'll show you how to be your own god in one easy step!" So instead of obeying God, Eve decided (by an act of her *will*) to be her own god.

Now, let's add what we've found out about Satan's three-part strategy, and bring our "world" study up to date:

"The World": Manipulated by Satan through an Invisible System—by Appealing to a Person's Physical Desires, Ego, or Will

Think through that statement about 13 times. It's as important as skis on a ski jumper for a Christian disciple to understand what the "world" is.

Now let's figure out how to apply our official statement about the "world" by seeing what's *worldly*:

• A kid is sitting on a bench at the mall while he waits for the pinball place to open. A girl in a sexy dress slinks by. After he pops his eyeballs back in, the kid casually saunters along behind the girl to play mind games with her body. Now, what's "worldly"? Sitting and watching people pass by in the mall isn't the worldly part of the story. The kid is being worldly as he allows his physical desires to sizzle, as he gives in to the lust of the flesh.

• A racy dress hangs limp in a closet. Hanging there it's just a skimpy bunch of cloth. But suddenly a girl yanks the dress off its hanger and puts it on to flaunt her sex appeal. The cloth, the dress, is not worldly. It doesn't have out-of-control physical desires, a puffed-up ego, or a theme song of "I Did It My Way." The girl is being worldly as she lets her *ego* be manipulated by the Enemy, as she gives in to the "look-at-me" motto of worldliness.

• The neatly typed copy of a speech sits on a desk. No problems with the "world" yet. Then the student council president snatches the speech, leaps up to a podium, and spouts his message *in order to* dazzle every ear with his charm and wit. The guy's "ain't I something" attitude is worldly. The speech is just a pawn in his game of "let-Satan-manipulate-my-ego." He's *in* the world and, at this point, *of* the world.

• Great Aunt Gertie gives you $75 for your birthday. You figure she must be getting senile, but you jump at the chance to blow the bucks on whatever you want. A pesky little voice inside your head keeps saying: "Let the Lord use some of it. Give some to somebody." But you decide that *you'll* decide how and where to spend the money, regardless of what God or anybody else thinks. Welcome to the big, bad "world"! Your *will* has been successfully manipulated by Satan and his hit men. You've given in to the pride of life—the side of you that wants to pull all your own strings, to make all your own rules, to be your own god.

Being "Worldly": Allowing One's Physical Desires, Ego, or Will to be Manipulated by Satan through an Invisible System

Now, how about the term "worldliness"? Worldliness is a pattern, a lifestyle of being worldly, of being manipulated by Satan's system. So it's always sin. Is the Enemy consistently manipulating a person's physical desires, ego, or will? If so, that person has stepped into a lifestyle of worldliness.

What's Your "World" View?

Maybe you're like I used to be. I'd hear older Christians warn about the big, bad world. But I always thought they sounded like finicky schoolmarms clucking, "Tut, tut, children. Don't be naughty now."

If I'd understood the biblical definition of the "world," I'd have had more respect for the warnings:

Warning #1—Your personal Enemy is out to destroy you, and he'll use the world system to get at you.

Warning #2—The world system, with its invisible army of spiritual beings, is more powerful than you are.

Warning #3—If you have a body, an ego, or a will, the world system constantly has access to you—whether you're in a church or a pool hall, whether you're talking with a Christian or a non-Christian.

Warning #4—Because the world isn't *things* or *people*, you cannot avoid the world by just staying away from "secular" places or non-Christians.

So you're in the world, like it or not. And the world's after you. It's as if you're in the old movie *The Blob* where a greasy giant amoeba oozes under every door to suffocate you.

"Stop the world!" you gasp. "I want to:

a. get off!"

b. join the system!"

c.. none of the above

3
The World—Withdraw or Conform?

As the official retreat speaker I was supposed to know all the answers. And Andy had a good question: "But how do I handle temptation and stuff in the world when I really want to . . ." He gulped.

"You really want to what?" I could guess what he was going to say.

"When I really just want to go for it?"

Good question, Andy. And there's no pat answer.

Andy was struggling with one of the most common responses people make to the world. He was on the verge of ignoring the Bible's warning about not fitting into the world's mold (Romans 12:2). He was probably so up to his neck in the world system that he just wanted to roll with the flow, try to be *in* the world and *of* it. Most people feel that way at one time or another.

Go for It!

If Andy did decide to jump into a world-system lifestyle, he'd have a variety of styles to choose from. For example:

The Mexican fisherman nodded and said, "Now I show you the delicacies of a man of the world!" And he slit the still-kicking sea turtle's throat. My daughter Ami and I stood on the beach beside the Sea of Cortez and waited for our lesson in how to "grab the gusto." The fisherman drained the blood into a pan. He offered a gulp to Ami (who politely mumbled, "No thank you"), and then chugged the entire potful of warm, fresh turtle blood himself. With a rattling belch, he concluded, "That, *mi amigo*, is livin' on top of the world!"

I learned another variation on the worldly lifestyle from Flynn, a spaced-out drug user I once worked with in a warehouse. "It's beautiful, man. You just float along, man. And, man, I was in the, you know. I was like in the ultimate. I realized what it's all about. Lyin' there in my bed I was seein' the sun. And then these beautiful clouds came up, man. And then this rain started pourin' down, man. . . ."

I was trying to count a billing order. "Yeah, well, what happened then, Flynn?"

"Well, I got up fast, man, cause I, uh, wet my bed. You know?"

So there are any number of world-system fans who will tell you how a real man or woman of the world should act. But the ways of the world all come together in three areas. Remember? If you want to go for a world-system lifestyle, you have to arrange your life around your physical desires, your ego, or your be-your-own god complex.

Invisible Strength

Keep in mind that it's not just the obviously sinful actions that conform people to the world system. The real strength of worldliness is in attitudes, values, and thoughts such as—

- praying a glorious prayer while feeling proud that your voice sounds so impressive;
- going out with somebody just to get some sensual kicks;
- saving the $8 in your pocket so you can buy an album, when you know your neighbor needs food but can't afford it;
- bragging about your musical, athletic, or academic abilities as if God hadn't given them to you;
- not associating with someone because he's not in with the right crowd.

It sounds pretty easy to conform to the world, doesn't it? It's downright natural. But remember, the Christian is a *super*natural person. He's been given a new nature. He's a brand-new person inside: "If any man is in Christ, he is a new creature" (2 Corinthians 5:17). So when the disciple of Jesus tries to "go for it," to grab the world's lifestyle, the results can be painful. Consider a couple of conditions that can develop.

Reverse Hypocrisy

Many people think of a hypocrite as someone who does the right things on the outside but whose heart is mean and nasty. Jesus' number one enemies, the scribes and Pharisees, practiced this type of hypocrisy (Matthew 23). But there's another type. And it's practiced by the Christian who conforms to the world system. Even though he lives a mean, nasty, and worldly lifestyle, his true nature is "created in righteousness and holiness" (Ephesians 4:24). His lifestyle is kind of a reverse hypocrisy—being a Christian inside, but living like the world.

According to the Bible, a Christian who lives as if he's part of the world system is like nonsalty salt. That kind of salt would obviously be good for nothing. Nobody would sprinkle it on food. It would be "useless either for the soil or for the manure pile" (Luke 14:35).

In the same way, a worldly Christian is useless to himself, to others around him, and to God. He tries to forget God, but can't because God's Spirit lives within him. He tries to enjoy sin, but the Holy Spirit convicts him. He tries to live a go-with-the-flow lifestyle, but the consequences of his sin make him miserable. He's like a fruit tree branch that never bears fruit (John 15:1-8); he's never satisfied because the purposes he was designed for aren't being fulfilled.

A Christian who tries to fit in with the world system never really feels at home there. The pleasures of the world finally leave him feeling empty—a victim of his hypocrisy.

Passing Through

Another result of conforming to the world can be found in 1 John 2:15. "Do not love the world, nor the things in the world. If anyone loves the world, the love of the Father is not in him." Now, God doesn't quit loving the person who grabs on to a world-system lifestyle. But His love can't operate the way it's supposed to in a Christian who conforms to the world. The more a person loves the world, the less he experiences God's love flowing through him.

While I was working on an offshore oil rig in the Gulf of Mexico, one of my jobs was to operate a survey tool. Suspended on a metal wire, this heavy piece of equipment zipped up and down in the hole which we had drilled to find oil.

One day I had run the tool down to about three miles and started bringing it back up when I noticed a crewman wrapping a rag around the wire. Evidently he was trying to clean the wire as it came out of the hole. Suddenly, the rag caught on the wire and whipped through a pulley. The wire snapped.

Screaming, I grabbed the broken wire to keep the heavy tool from falling to the bottom of the hole. But the tool was too heavy; I couldn't hold on. As the wire slid through my hands, I could feel them burning, even though I was wearing gloves.

I was about to let go of the wire when I noticed the steel brace in front of me. Somehow I managed to maneuver the wire till it kinked around the brace, giving just enough added support so that I was able to hold on till help came.

The episode ended with me still holding on to the kinked wire while the boss screamed and cursed the crew into remounting the pulley. I held the wire for about five minutes till my fingers went numb and my arms started doing the rhumba. Pretty soon I couldn't feel the wire at all. While the wire was passing through my hands, I definitely felt it. When it wasn't passing through, I couldn't feel a thing.

In a similar way, when God's love is moving through you, you sense it. It affects others, so you see it. But when you conform your lifestyle to the world system, the love of the Father doesn't pass through anymore. He still loves you, but you don't feel His love. You start to wonder whether God cares about you at all. You have trouble loving other people. You *feel* as if your relationship with God has ended. Ever felt that way? It's the feeling that comes when you try to love the world, to conform to the world.

Let's face it. "Going for it," trying to fit into the world system's mold, is not worth it. "Do not be conformed to this world" (Romans 12:2). Conforming is no way for a disciple to respond to the world he's *in* but not of.

Run from It!

There's another way that Christians respond to the world system. I call it the Quarantine Method. Fans of this approach figure, "Since all non-Christians are contaminated with worldliness, stay away from them. Stay away from everything they do. Be an *out*-of-this-world disciple!"

Sometimes the "out-of-this-world crowd" uses the Bible to support its run-and-hide approach. The argument usually goes something like this: "The Bible teaches Christians to keep themselves 'unstained by the world' (James 1:27). God also says Christians should 'come out from their midst and be separate' (2 Corinthians 6:17). So, if 'secular' things and non-Christian people are worldly, well then, Christians should just keep away from all non-sacred things and all non-Christian people!"

It's as simple as that. Simple—and wrong. The real error behind the Quarantine Method is that it's based on a false understanding of what worldliness really is.

Jesus prayed to God the Father, "I do not ask Thee to take them out of the world, but to keep them from the evil one . . . . As Thou didst send Me into the world, I also have sent them into the world" (John 17:15, 18).

Christian records and concerts are good ideas. Christian schools are very good ideas. Christian radio and TV stations are too. Any of these ministries are fine—as long as they don't *isolate* Christians from the world. But as my friend Al once said in jest, "Just think, I can do all my business, take all my schooling, listen to the radio, watch TV, read thousands of books, and have all kinds of fun without ever having to even talk to a non-Christian." As Al knew, withdrawing from the world, like conforming to the world, can cause lots of problems.

Cold Turkey

One symptom that turns up when Christians isolate themselves from the world is *fear*—fear of the unknown. Pollyanna Pureheart has never had a non-Christian friend, never watched a non-sacred TV show, never talked with a guy who rides motorcycles. And Polly is afraid. She's afraid of striking up a conversation with a real, live heathen. She's afraid to think through what's good about a secular book, and what's bad. She's afraid to attend a state university. An isolated Christian can easily become afraid of the non-Christian world.

Another result of the run-from-it strategy is *ineffectiveness*. A disciple who is afraid of people in the world is often a dud when it comes to reaching out with Christ's love. Have you ever known a preacher or a Christian teacher who was so isolated from the world that he just couldn't relate to real people? Obviously, if you're not rubbing shoulders with the people of the world, you seldom find openings to share Christ with them. You don't know how to talk with them, much less reach them.

What I call a *flat lifestyle* is another result of being isolated from the world. Mostly, such a lifestyle is flat because it's not the true lifestyle of discipleship. But more specifically, it's flat because it offers few challenges. To be isolated is to be like a lion tamer who never steps in with the lions. It's like a war hero who never goes to battle. It's like an athlete who never enters a competition.

If you find no challenge in your life as a Christian disciple, it could be because you've copped out of the fight. You're not facing the world, so you don't feel the need to depend on God for strength.

Disciples who pretend to live *out* of the world often attend lots of dull meetings and drag through plenty of meaningless religious exercises. But there's nothing really challenging or rewarding about their Christian lives. Everything's *flat*.

Finally, the Quarantine Method means that an isolated Christian misses so much. So many rewarding relationships, great ideas, and exciting activities are just crossed off his list because he thinks they're evil when they may not be at all!

Running from the world isn't the answer. The world system isn't people. Or certain objects. Even if a disciple stays away from all non-Christians, stays isolated from all the products and activities and ideas of the non-Christian world, that world still saturates his environment.

Because the world is invisible, it can creep into the most secluded monastery. It's true. Even monks have to contend with Satan's attempts to manipulate their physical desires, their egos, and their wills. A Christian kid who attends a Christian school and has only Christian friends who enjoy only Christian activities can be as *worldly* as anyone. Running from the world—isolationism—doesn't work.

The World a Winner?

So what does work? If *going for it* guarantees a disastrous lifestyle for the disciple, and if *running from* the world promises only more problems, what's the answer? How can a disciple live *in* the world and yet not be *of* the world?

There really is an answer. If you're feeling like the big, bad world is just too bad for any disciple to handle, don't give up yet. Stick with me while we figure out what Jesus really meant when He said His disciples are to be "not of this world, *even as I am not of this world*" (John 17:14, italics mine).

4
Discernment in the World

"You can't get a clean banana out of a dirty garbage can," so the old saying goes. It's a good old saying—except when applied to true Christianity. That's because God *can* get a clean banana out of a dirty garbage can. It *is* possible to be a pure, clean disciple while living in a nasty world—without running or conforming. A person can live *in* the world without being *of* it.

Let's call this genuinely Christian response to the world *discernment*. Having discernment means having the *wisdom* to know what's of the world and what's not. It means having the *ability* to reject what's worldly and to accept what's not of the world.

Want to see how discernment can work in some real-life, "garbage-can" situations? Just take a look at how Jesus handled the big, bad world:

"As Jesus passed on from there, He saw a man, called Matthew, sitting in the tax office; and He said to him, 'Follow Me!' And he rose, and followed Him. And it happened that as He was reclining at table in the house, behold many tax-gatherers and sinners came and joined Jesus and His disciples at the table. And when the Pharisees saw this, they said to His disciples, 'Why does your Teacher eat with the tax-gatherers and sinners?' But when He heard this, He said, 'It is not those who are healthy who need a physician, but those who are ill. But go and learn what this means, "I desire compassion, and not sacrifice," for I did not come to call the righteous, but sinners' " (Matthew 9:9-13).

Another time, Jesus spoke of how the religious leaders had branded Him with a bad reputation: "The Son of man came eating and drinking, and they say, 'Behold a gluttonous man and a drunkard, a friend of tax-gatherers and sinners!' " (Matthew 11:19)

If you've ever heard Christians talk about being "separate from the world," you may have thought that being "separate" means practicing the Quarantine Method of staying away from non-Chris-

tians. But let's look closely at Jesus' style of
separation:

- His Word commands, "Come out from them
  and be separate" (2 Corinthians 6:17, NIV).
- Yet Jesus rubbed shoulders with sinners; He
  was criticized for socializing with the low life
  of Palestine (Matthew 11:19).
- And yet Jesus is praised as holy, undefiled,
  and "separated from sinners" (Hebrews 7:26).

Jesus was perfectly *separated*, yet He associ-
ated openly with unbelievers. So God's idea of
being separate can't be simply *physical* separation
from non-Christians or from "secular" things. Biblical separation means not giving in to the lust of
the flesh, the lust of the eyes, or the pride of life—
regardless of how good or bad your surroundings
may be. Jesus lived a perfect life of separation—
separation not from the *people* of the world, but
from the *sin* of the world system. He lived *in* the
world but He wasn't overcome *by* it. In fact, He
clearly said, "Take courage; I have overcome the
world" (John 16:33).

But, you're thinking, *that's fine for Jesus. He's
God. He can handle anything. He has the wisdom
to decide what's worldly and what isn't—when
to get involved and when to draw the line. And
He has the ability not to go over the line once it's
drawn—not to get enticed into sin.*

If that's what you're thinking, you're way ahead
of me. Jesus does have the wisdom and ability to
live with discernment in the world, to neither *go
for it* nor *run from it*. He can overcome the world.
And that's just the point. He can. You can't. Stay
with me, OK?

The Spirit Is Willing

Though Jesus is now seated at the right hand of the Father (Ephesians 1:18-23), His Spirit lives in every born-again disciple! If you belong to Christ, you have the Spirit of Christ *in* you (Romans 8:9). Get a hold of this: The same Holy Spirit that lived in the physical body of Jesus while He was on earth lives now in the physical bodies of Jesus' disciples! The Spirit that supplied Jesus' *wisdom* and *ability* to live in but not of the world is also available to you as a disciple!

The wisdom. With the Spirit's help, you don't have to conform to the world or to run scared from it. Your Spirit-guided discernment can help you overcome the world: "Whatever is born of God overcomes the world; and this is the victory that has overcome the world—our faith. And who is the one who overcomes the world, but he who believes that Jesus is the Son of God?" (1 John 5:4-5)

What is it about Jesus' disciples that overcomes the world? It's their faith. And where does faith come from? "Faith comes from hearing, and hearing by the Word of Christ" (Romans 10:17). The Word of Christ, the Bible, is the source of discerning *wisdom*. The Bible can teach today's disciples how to figure out what's righteous and what's worldly.

But how does the typical Joe Disciple understand the Bible? Again here's where the Holy Spirit comes in: "Now we have received, not the spirit of the world, but the Spirit who is from God, that we might know the things freely given to us by God . . . in [words] taught by the Spirit, combining spiritual thoughts with spiritual words" (1 Corinthians 2:12-13). The Holy Spirit will guide Jesus' disciples into truth (John 16:13) by helping them understand God's Word.

The ability. Along with learning Spirit-controlled wisdom from the Bible, there's a second step in developing a discerning lifestyle. Step two is coming up with the *ability* to act on the wisdom. Where does the ability come from? It too comes from the Holy Spirit: "You shall receive *power* when the Holy Spirit has come upon you" (Acts 1:8, italics mine). "In order that the requirement of the Law might be fulfilled in us, who do not walk according to the flesh, but according to the Spirit" (Romans 8:4).

As a disciple allows Christ to control his life, something amazing happens. The same Spirit who gave power to Jesus while He was on earth also gives power to His disciple. With the Spirit's power, even the weakest disciple can overcome the world system. However, this ability doesn't come from the disciple at all, but from the Holy Spirit working in the disciple's life.

So you live *in* the world but not *of* the world by taking these two steps: *Step A*—use Spirit-controlled wisdom in deciding what's of the world and what's not. *Step B*—use your Spirit-controlled ability to reject what's of the world and accept what isn't. As you walk in the power of Christ's Spirit, you can live the right kind of separation and say with the Apostle Paul, "The world is a dead thing to me and I am a dead man to the world!" (Galatians 6:14, PH)

Life in the Garbage Can

You want to figure out whether or not to watch a certain TV show. To read a new book by a famous author. To listen to certain music. To play a certain game. The *go for it* person would say, "Sure, go for it. Don't worry about it." The *run from it* isolationist would say a simple, "No, no, no!" to all of these situations. After all, falling back on a human rule such as "Thou Shalt Not Listen to Popular Music" or "Thou Shalt Not Read Any Secular Literature" is a lot easier than trusting the Holy Spirit to provide discernment!

Every day brings new decisions that require Spirit-guided discernment. You have to decide. Will you be worldly—of the world—if you watch, read, listen, play, or participate?

Smokers' Corner

Let's try some case studies:

At the beginning of the school year, Betty Buskowsky didn't have a single non-Christian friend. She decided it was because she was an isolated Christian. So just to make contact with a few pagans, Betty started hanging around with the girls at Smokers' Corner. Betty thought: *Maybe I can get to know some of the girls well enough to share my faith with them.*

One day the old lady who owned the yard on Smokers' Corner started shrieking and running after the girls with a broom because they were leaving cigarette butts all over her lawn. The girls reacted in their usual super-cool way. "Drop dead, you old bat!" they yelled. Betty was the only one who tried to apologize to the old lady.

After the angry woman stomped back into the house, one of the girls sat down next to Betty. "You were right," the girl said. "She's really an OK old bat. I think you were right to apologize to her."

Yahoo! thought Betty, *I'm being accepted!*

"By the way, I never see you smoke," said the girl. "Got no cigarettes? Or are you into the heavier stuff?"

"Yrouafgh," mumbled Betty.

"Here." The girl reached into her purse and snaked out a joint. All the girls noticed. They realized that Betty was about to be officially accepted into the group. The girl held the match cupped in her hand while she sucked on the reefer. Then she spit out a seed and passed the joint to Betty.

Now, I know Betty's story reads like one of those adult-to-kid stories about "What Will Happen if You Hang Around with the Wrong Crowd." And usually, such a story concludes with the advice: "Stay away; then you won't be tempted." But let's look at this story a different way. Has Betty sinned yet? Though she stuck herself right in the middle of foreign territory, *in* the world, is she being worldly?

What's the situation? Betty is being offered a joint in front of a group of girls she wants to be friends with. Does the situation appeal to the lust of the flesh, the lust of the eyes, or the pride of life—the things that make up worldliness? Yep. Betty's ego is at stake. Her natural desire to look good, to fit in, is being appealed to. In other words, Betty is being tempted.

So how did Betty handle the big, bad world? Betty's Spirit-controlled study of God's Word helped her remember: "Your body is a temple of the Holy Spirit who is in you, whom you have from God, and . . . you are not your own. For you have been bought with a price: therefore glorify God in your body" (1 Corinthians 6:19-20). Betty had also read enough about smoking dope to know the physical/mental consequences of using marijuana. Wisdom told Betty it was time to draw the line.

SITUATION	WORLD'S APPEAL	RELEVANT SCRIPTURE	WORLDLY?
Hanging around Smokers' Corner		John 17:18	Not necessarily
Joint offered	to Betty's ego	1 Corinthians 6:19-20	If yielded to, yep!

Next, Betty had to trust the Holy Spirit to control her response in the situation.

"Not me, thanks," Betty replied to the girl. "Got to keep my brain straight."

The girl just nodded. "Wish I'd said that when my sister first got me into dope. I've got to keep in business now, though. Like, I can't really go more than a few days without getting good and stoned and—I know it sounds dumb—but don't get into it if you don't have to. You know? Sometimes I wish . . ."

Does Betty's story sound corny? Sorry. But it's based on something that actually happened to me in a different setting. I was in a situation just like Betty's. I found my ego being tempted *by* the world to be *of* the world. And when I said a shaky but simple, "No thanks," the guy offering the joint opened up like a tulip. He shared some of his own doubts and fears with me. So this "case study" may sound corny, but it raises some serious questions:

- Was Betty being worldly by hanging around Smokers' Corner?
- Was Betty being worldly in wanting to make friends with the girls?
- Was it to be expected that Betty's Christianity would be tested as she hung around with the girls?
- Would it have been easy for Betty to simply conform, to kick back and go for it when the world appealed to her ego?
- Would it have been easy for Betty to simply stay away from all those heathens?
- If Betty would have conformed or stayed away, would the girls have glimpsed the special quality in her that made her stand up for what was right and say no to what was wrong?
- Where did Betty draw the line between being *in* the world system and being *of* it?

As Betty's story illustrates, living *in* but not *of* the world is risky business. There are temptations. There is a regular smorgasbord of appeals to your physical desires, your ego, and your be-your-own-god complex. But being tempted doesn't mean you've done wrong or that you're worldly. It's when you give in to the temptation that worldliness gets you.

But you don't have to give in to worldliness even when surrounded by it. "Do not go on presenting the members of your body to sin as instruments of unrighteousness; but present yourselves to God as those alive from the dead, and your members as instruments of righteousness to God" (Romans 6:13). Remember? Whether you're being worldly or godly is a question of who you let control you—Satan or God.

I Spy

Ray sprawled beside the pool and opened the new spy novel. He switched on the radio. Within minutes his head was brimming with dark, sneaky meetings, a stiletto stabbing, espionage, and counter-espionage. Then, about chapter 3, the girl showed up. (Spy novels always seem to have the girl showing up about chapter 3.) There were two quick paragraphs describing her body and then the story ran back into its web of secretive schemes. Ray skimmed over the paragraphs remembering the Bible's instructions to "Flee youthful lusts" (2 Timothy 2:22). When he'd gotten past the racy part, Ray went on to enjoy the rest of the story.

As he got into chapter 4, he stopped to listen to a song on the radio: "Do your own thing; yeah, do your own thing; no matter what they tell ya . . ."

"Wrong," Ray said, and switched stations. He

remembered some other words: "You shall have no other gods before Me" (Exodus 20:3).

Was our man Ray being worldly? The racy parts of the book were designed to appeal to the lust of the flesh, Ray's physical desires. As Ray's eyes telegraphed the works to his brain, he was being tempted; his physical desires were being appealed to. But remember where the line between being *in* and *of* the world is drawn? It's drawn at the line of sin, at the point of yielding to temptation. And only Ray and God know if Ray yielded, if he played mind games with the racy description he skimmed over. Hopefully, he recognized the appeal of the world, rejected it, and went on in discernment to appreciate the rest of the novel.

Likewise, the ideas presented in the song on the radio contradicted Ray's understanding of God's commandment. So he rejected the ideas. He squinted with Spirit-guided wisdom at the baloney that was being played. Then he used his Spirit-powered ability to switch stations.

- Is reading a secular novel worldly?
- Would it have been easy for Ray to ponder over the racy part of the book, to give in to its lust-of-the-flesh appeal by playing sensual mind games?
- Would Ray be better off if he never read a secular book?
- Is listening to secular songs on the radio worldly?
- Is a person who listens to a song on the radio being worldly if he decides to agree with or act on the false ideas in the song?
- Would Ray be better off if he never listened to any secular music?

SITUATION	WORLD'S APPEAL	RELEVANT SCRIPTURE	WORLDLY?
Reading a spy novel	to Ray's physical desires	2 Timothy 2:22	If yielded to, yep!
Listening to a song with worldly lyrics	to Ray's be-your-own-god complex	Exodus 20:3	If accepted, yep!

Danger!

I can just feel the panic rising in the parents and youth workers who read this chapter. And it's a justifiable panic. Practicing discernment in the world can be dangerous. But learning to be a discerning disciple is, in the long run, "safer" than being a run-and-hide Christian.

When young Christians don't practice Spirit-controlled discernment, Christian authorities often try to keep them from dangerous temptations with warnings such as: "Don't listen to secular music. Don't read secular books. Don't look at secular art. Don't wear clothes styles that are up to date. Don't have any non-Christian friends. No. No. No."

Someone who says to you, "Stay away from the world," is really saying, "I care about you. I don't want you to be destroyed." But as we saw in the last chapter, staying away from the externals of worldliness doesn't make you godly inside. And it somehow fools you into feeling that you don't need to practice Spirit-controlled discernment. The dangers involved in practicing discernment shouldn't push Christians into isolation.

On the other hand, remember that the world will tempt you to be worldly (Proverbs 1:10; 24:1-2; Ephesians 5:5-12). Every disciple should be aware of the dangers that go along with a lifestyle of discernment. Be careful.

Warning #1. This discernment idea doesn't mean you can just jump into anything and then, on the way down, "discern" what's wrong with it.

There are lots of situations and activities that must be avoided—period. For example, there's not a chance that you could murder, hate, have sex with someone you're not married to, lie, get drunk, cheat, or steal without immediately being *Of* the world—with a capital *O*. That's because these activities are listed in the Bible as sin. Flat-out sin.

There's no way you can pretend to practice discernment (rejecting what's worldly) when you're out-and-out sinning. The *biblical* (as opposed to many of the *traditional*) no-no's are set, constant, and God-ordered.

Warning #2. Another danger of using discernment in the world comes from plain old human weakness.

There's a saying that goes, "It's the little foxes that spoil the vine" (Song of Solomon 2:15, paraphrased). The idea is that your relationship with God is threatened more by the small, everyday temptations than by the biggies. For example, you sit down in a coffeehouse—being in the world but not of it—and a junkie comes over and asks, "Want a quick fix, man?" Chances are you won't fall across the table to give in to temptation. It's more likely that over a period of time as you run into kids who use drugs, you'll give in to one small area of temptation. Then another, then another. Until you're not only totally *in* the world—you've become *of* it too.

It's sort of like the experiment where a frog won't stay in a pan of hot water, but he'll stay in a pan of cool water that is gradually heated—till he boils to death. You've *got* to be alert to the little, gradual temptations as you live in the world.

While I was writing this book a kid in my town died sitting in his parked pickup. He wasn't a bad kid. He just got into the wrong little things. He smoked a lot of marijuana. He got into sniffing cans of that nonstick cooking stuff. The autopsy revealed that his death was probably caused by an overdose of heroin. Did he plan it that way? Nope. Just as Christians never plan to end up on dope, to end up in emotional pain, to commit suicide, to live twisted lives sexually, to become bitter, sick, and ugly inside. But it happens when a disciple depends on his own strength to resist the steady, gradual pull of the world.

Sometimes it's best to avoid areas where you have been especially weak, where you've often given in to temptation, where you have trouble letting the Spirit control you. If you're an alcoholic, be sensitive to the fact that the Lord may want you to avoid places where alcohol is served. If you've been sexually loose with somebody, it's probably best that you quit going out with that person. If certain music triggers an old sense of depression in you, quit listening. Don't isolate yourself from the world altogether, but then *don't think it's a cop-out to stay away from specific areas of temptation where you're likely to bomb out.*

Never rush into the world's domain without a thorough grasp of how God, working in you, can resist temptation. The Bible verse isn't, "Greater are you than he that is in the world." It's, "Greater is He who is in you than he who is in the world" (1 John 4:4). Don't kid yourself. You're weak. Only Jesus living in you by the Spirit is strong.

Warning #3. Sometimes the authorities in your life will determine whether an activity is worldly for you or not. Think carefully with me:

You're chosen as a runner-up for homecoming court. The queen and her court are expected to reign over the school year's biggest formal dance. You pray and your discernment tells you that you can attend the thing without giving in to worldliness. You're positive that you can be a Christian *in* the world but not *of* it at the event. But Ma and Pa think otherwise. They say, "No go."

Guess what? If you go in spite of your parents' objections, you're being worldly! Worldliness will grab you even before you set foot in the dance because you're violating a command of God: "Children, obey your parents" (Ephesians 6:1). If you go, you're saying to yourself: "Self, my parents are simply strange. Forget them and forget God's ideas about them. I have a better idea than God. I'll disobey them and disobey Him—and not be worldly at the dance at all!" And Satan, manipulating the *pride of life*, has already pulled you right into the world system.

God's command concerning obedience to authorities takes priority over a disciple's personal discernment.

On Being a Clean Banana

This has been a pretty heavy chapter. You'd do well to read and think it through several times. Discernment in discipleship is just that crucial. Remember the keys to discernment: Spirit-guided *wisdom* from the Bible to know what worldliness is, and Spirit-powered *ability* to resist giving in to worldliness.

Make out a chart like the two in this chapter to help you in your own discernment process. Pick one simple activity and work it through on the chart. Practice discernment even before you're involved in a risky situation.

And be prepared for the risk, for the temptation. Learn how to be a clean banana in a garbage-can world—by mastering God's beat-the-system strategy of discernment.

5 Temptation in the World

Blood poured down Shelly's arm from the gouge in her wrist. She tried to slash the other wrist, but her wounded arm was too unsteady. The butcher knife dropped to the floor as Shelly began to pass out.

She woke, the wound having clotted while she lay unconscious on the dirt floor of a hut in the Guatemalan jungle. Shelly lived to tell her story of temptation:

"I was always overweight. The real reason I went to the mission field was because I thought I was too unattractive to be important for God in the U.S. So I wound up as a single missionary thousands of miles from home, and I got depressed.

"My ministry was a total bomb. The men wouldn't listen to me and the women were told to stay away. I worked and prayed with a few children, but even they wouldn't respond to my stories about Jesus. The depression got to be overwhelming. It got so bad that I'd just sit in my house all day. Then the monsoon rainy season came and for days at a time, I never saw another missionary. I was completely isolated because of the mud and rain-swollen rivers. It was about that time that thoughts of suicide started hounding me.

"I never thought of suicide as a temptation, but that's what it was. It was as if Satan himself were saying to me, 'You are worthless. You're no good to these people. You're no good to yourself and no good to God. You've got no reason for being alive. You're worthless.'

"I guess I gave in to the thoughts. I gave in to the temptation to believe that God didn't care about me anymore, that I should just end it. So that's when I tried to use the butcher knife. Thank God, He let me live!"

In Shelly's case, temptation attacked by manipulating her *be-your-own-god complex*. Her temptation was to believe that God didn't really love her, and that she should play God by taking her own life.

Shelly's experience is unique, but it underscores the fact that living in the world can be a risky business. Everyone who lives *in* the world system is sometimes tempted to be *of* the world system—tempted to sin.

The Problem

Whenever someone receives Christ, that person becomes a "new creature" (2 Corinthians 5:17). He becomes a brand-new person inside. And that *new self* is "created in righteousness and holiness" (Ephesians 4:24). But as long as he lives on this earth, the Christian's new self must contend with the old self that's so easily attracted to sin. So temptation for a disciple is a built-in problem.

The Attraction

There's a takeoff on the old Gospel hymn, "Love Lifted Me," that goes: "I was sinking deep in sin. . . . Yahoo!" It's not a very reverent way to treat a beautiful hymn, but the revised version makes a point: The Christian's old self likes sin!

"The flesh sets its desire against the Spirit" (Galatians 5:17). The word *desire* here has a more intense meaning in the original language of the Bible. It means "a deep craving." In other words, the disciple's old self deeply craves the opposite of what the Spirit in the disciple's new self wants. The Spirit-controlled new self doesn't want to give in to the temptations of the world system. But— and how well we all know it—the old self craves to give in.

As long as the disciple allows the Spirit to control him, he doesn't have to give in to temptation.

But when a Christian stops relying on the Spirit for strength, he is no longer able to withstand the temptations of the world system. The world offers up all kinds of sinful treats which appeal to the lust of the flesh, the lust of the eyes, and the pride of life (1 John 2:16). And the old self croons, "My favorites!"

When the old self is in control, it's easy to delight in wickedness (2 Thessalonians 2:12), and to "enjoy the pleasures of sin for a short time" (Hebrews 11:25, NIV). Even for a disciple, it can somehow feel natural to just slip-slide your way into worldliness.

Sin is always deceptive that way. It always looks so good in the temptation stage. Since "Satan disguises himself as an angel of light" (2 Corinthians 11:14), it's no big deal for him to make the stinkiest of his world-system schemes appear as harmless as apple pie. Just think of some of the TV commercials that push worldly products and lifestyles, like the ads featuring a party at a Playboy mansion for example. Lavish food, the best in music, suave gentlemen, and shapely ladies—it looks like "the good life." So sophisticated. So chic. So much fun.

Sin in the world system looks attractive because of its deceptive appeal to the deep cravings of the old self. Christ's disciples are surrounded by an attractive, tempting system of sin. The attractions of the world are an unavoidable fact of life.

The Ingredients

"Each one is tempted when, by his own evil desire, he is dragged away and enticed" (James 1:14,

NIV). Temptation has two main ingredients: a person's own evil desires or cravings, and an enticement. The cravings of the old self can be thought of as a keg of gunpowder. The enticement of sin is like a match. So guess what happens when the two get together.

If you find yourself being blasted by one temptation after the other, don't feel like the Lone Ranger. I once spoke at a camp where a group of churchgoing kids anonymously listed temptations they had given in to during the year leading up to the camp. Here's part of that list:

I started smoking dope this year.
I stole some money from my mother.
I cheated.
I went to bed with my boyfriend.
I stole money from my parents.
I started on speed and coke and I have some with me this week.
I got my girlfriend in trouble.
I had an abortion and I can't forget it.
I messed around with the wrong crowd.
I was arrested for dealing.
I gave up my virginity.
I started smoking and swearing.
I lied to my folks.
I lied to so many people I can't even remember who.

Add to the list the less spectacular sins of having a critical spirit, refusing to forgive, worrying, being hateful, deceiving, lusting—and we'd have a pretty good summary of the types of temptations disciples have to deal with.

Battle Tactics

Temptation is the special work of that very organized group known as "the rulers . . . the powers . . . the world forces of this darkness, and the spiritual forces of wickedness in the heavenly places" (Ephesians 6:12). Remember? They're the ones who control the invisible world system. A battle with temptation is no friendly little street brawl. You're up against an *army* of evil. Temptation is warfare, not a dainty Ping-Pong match. So you need to understand some basic military strategy.

For instance, you need to know your firepower. Fortunately, the *ability* to fight temptation doesn't come from ourselves. Remember the last chapter on discernment? As we give in to God the Spirit, He provides the firepower. "You shall receive power when the Holy Spirit has come upon you" (Acts 1:8). The word "power" in this verse is the Greek word *dunamin* from which we get the English word "dynamite"! So we've got plenty of firepower. The dynamite-power available to us is unlimited!

So much for our weapons. You ought to be an expert by now on how God's powerful Spirit lives His life in your new nature. Next, what kind of tactics do we plot? Where and how does the Enemy attack? What's our defense plan? The answers can be found in our battle plan, the Bible.

The Attack

Where does the attack come? Where are the enticements of sin aimed? You guessed it. The Enemy attacks today's disciples in the same three areas in which he tempted Eve (Genesis 3:1-6). He appeals to physical desires, the ego, and the desire to be your own god.

The *desires of the body* are a prime target for enemy attack. You're tempted to pervert the innocent biological desires of enjoying married sex, of eating good food, and of resting into sexual impurity, gluttony, and laziness. Satan says, "This will make you *feel* so good!" And you're tempted to surrender your physical drives to your old self to be used in sin.

King David faced a temptation in the area of his body as the Enemy appealed to his physical drives. (This is the episode that starts with Bathsheba in the bath. See 2 Samuel 11.) Now, there's nothing wrong with enjoying beauty, and nothing wrong with the biological desire for sexual relations. But when "enjoying beauty" becomes lust, and the desire for sex becomes adultery, the lighted powder keg of temptation blows up, as it did in David's situation. Read Psalm 51 to discover how this great man of God reacted when he bombed out to a temptation of his body.

Temptation also attacks by appealing to your *ego*. Satan says, "This will make you *look* so good!" And you're tempted to protect your ego. The devil sings to your desire to be important with tunes such as, "You're not goin' to be chicken, are ya?" or "C'mon, everybody's going to be there!" or "What are you—weird?" Some results of giving in to the temptations of your ego are becoming a "Secret Service Christian," cheating for better grades, gossiping, and swearing.

Good old Apostle Peter provides the perfect example of a disciple who surrendered to temptation in this area (Luke 22:54-62). Luke describes how Peter denied Christ when a little girl accused him of being a disciple. While Jesus was being tried inside a nearby building, the girl said to Peter, "You're one of those strange Christians!" And Peter, rock of Christendom, said something like, "!#★!!★%#!!! I am not!" He buckled under the pressure of the world system in order to preserve his ego.

Finally, temptation attacks by appealing to your *be-your-own-god complex*, by twisting your concept of the real God. The Enemy croons, "You don't need God; be god yourself! He doesn't really love you. He doesn't really mean what He says. He won't take care of you." You're tempted to alter your idea of who God is, to quit trusting in Him.

Eve's story illustrates this area of temptation (Genesis 3:1-6). Remember? Satan suggested that Eve could be her own god, knowing good and evil, flaunting God's commandments. So Eve reached up in the forbidden tree, grabbed a banana and munched. (It could have been a banana, you know.) Read the rest of Genesis 3 which tells what happened after Eve's defeat. It wasn't a pretty story. It still isn't.

Tactical Defense

Now, time to plot a defense. The Bible story of Joseph illustrates how to defend against a temptation that appeals to your *physical desires*. The wife of Joseph's boss tried to get Joseph to go to bed with her (Genesis 39). Faced with this temp-

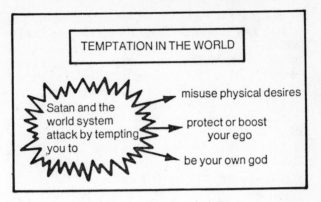

tation, Joseph hotfooted it out of the situation. He took off so fast that the woman was left holding his cloak—making Joseph Egypt's first streaker! Joseph's defense is sometimes known as the "flee tactic" because of the New Testament reference, "Flee from youthful lusts" (2 Timothy 2:22).

When the sight of barely dressed bodies at the beach tempts you to sin by playing sexual mind games, get up and run five miles down the beach! Go play tennis instead! Get yourself out of the situation that tempts you physically.

Another Bible story, found in Numbers 14:1-14, 38, contains the perfect defense against temptation that attacks the *ego*. Moses had sent out a group of men to spy out the land of Canaan. When the men returned, all but two of them reported that the Canaanites were just too strong to conquer. When the people heard the report, they got angry with Moses and decided to appoint a new leader and go back to Egypt.

But there were two spies who stood up to give a different report. Joshua and Caleb said, "Hey, we can do it. God will be with us. Let's take Canaan!" Tempted to protect their egos, to go along with the crowd, Joshua and Caleb rebelled against the crowd instead of rebelling against God.

Joshua and Caleb were illustrating a New Testament defense tactic: "Do not love the world, nor the things in the world. If anyone loves the world, the love of the Father is not in him" (1 John 2:15). Loving is not a feeling of attraction. It is, biblically, a decision to serve. If you decide to serve the world system (which hates Christians, remember—John 15:19), you rebel against God (who loves you—John 15:9). If you decide to serve God, you rebel against the world. And that's exactly the tactic Joshua and Caleb used when world-system peer pressure tempted their egos to conform. They decided to rebel against the crowd's view rather than to rebel against God (Numbers 14:9).

When you're tempted to take a toke, to snub a loser because everybody's watching, to flaunt your sexuality so you'll be noticed, to guzzle Mad Dog wine because everybody else is, to deny being a disciple of Jesus—make a decision to *rebel* against what the world wants you to do. Maybe even say it verbally: "I don't have to drink just because everybody else is." Get the idea? You can be free of world-manipulation by deciding to rebel against the world and to serve God.

In a strange spiritual encounter, Michael the archangel used a powerful weapon against a temptation aimed at his *be-your-own-god-complex*. Knowing that direct spiritual combat against Satan was too tough even for an archangel, Michael said to Satan, "The Lord rebuke you!" (Jude 9) Michael used the defense tactic found in James 4:7—"Submit therefore to God. Resist the devil and he will flee from you." It's a good phrase to remember: "Lord, rebuke Satan!"

When you feel God's forgotten you, when you want to take things into your own hands instead of waiting on Him, when you think God's ideas aren't as good as yours, when you think God blew it when He designed you—pray something like, "Lord, get Satan with his ideas away from me, in the name of Jesus Christ!" When you're tempted to be your own god, ask God to rebuke the Enemy.

Now let's look at a chart of our tactical defenses:

AREA OF ATTACK	DEFENSIVE TACTIC
Physical desires	Flee the situation (2 Timothy 2:22)
Ego	Rebel against the world system (1 John 2:15)
Be-your-own-god-complex	Ask God to rebuke Satan (Jude 9)

Application Time

We could look at how Jesus Himself used these three defense tactics when Satan tempted Him (Luke 4:1-13). Remember? First, the Enemy tempted Jesus to turn stones into bread for His hungry body. Then Satan tempted Christ to feed His ego by becoming the instant ruler of the world. Finally, the devil tempted Jesus to put God to the test by doing a swan dive off the top of the temple.

We could also talk about Jesus' victory over temptation (Hebrews 2:18; 4:15). Or, we could talk about how to use these defense tactics in our everyday lives in the world. But, instead, let's leave the application of these tactics to this little multiple-choice quiz:

1. When you're alone in the house, and your date nuzzles your ear and whispers, "Let's go check out the bedroom, *mon cheri*," you:
   a. kneel by the bedside, raise your hands in prayer, and shout, "O Lord, rebuke this here evil spirit!"
   b. jump to your feet and say, "Let's go get a pizza!"
2. When the kids at the other end of your park bench roll a joint and offer you a hit saying, "You're not one of those straights, are you?":
   a. you leap into a sprinter's starting position and yell, "Runners, to your marks; get set . . . !"
   b. you smile and say, "Thanks. Don't need it."
3. When you—the only student who didn't cheat—flunk the final, and you think God's unfair, you:
   a. decide to phone the cheaters' names in as an anonymous tip to the FBI.
   b. pray that God will rebuke the enemy and his lies.

If you answered "b" to all of the above, congratulations—you haven't been sleeping through this chapter! But stay with me. There's one final tidbit you should know about temptation.

You're Peculiar

As a disciple of Jesus, you are a *peculiar* person. Not peculiar as in spacy or odd. You're peculiar as in—"The great God and our Saviour Jesus Christ ... gave Himself for us, that He might redeem us from all iniquity, and purify unto Himself a *peculiar* people, zealous of good works" (Titus 2:13-14, KJV, italics mine).

What's that got to do with temptation? The word translated *peculiar* comes from two Greek words meaning "to be" and "around." Visualize a dot with a great big circle drawn around it. You're the dot. God is the circle. He's all around you. You're peculiar to Him—you're a little dot in the middle of His circle. He owns you.

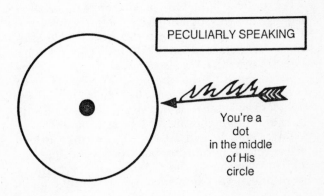

PECULIARLY SPEAKING

You're a
dot
in the middle
of His
circle

Now, imagine a fiery arrow (Ephesians 6:16) being launched toward the dot from outside the circle. It has to go through the circle before it can even hit the dot, right? A temptation won't hit you—the dot—till God has checked it out first. He lets in the ones He knows you can handle when you depend on the Spirit and use His defense tactics. He keeps out the temptations you just can't bear. Paul put it this way: "God is faithful; He will not let you be tempted beyond what you can bear. But when you are tempted, He will also provide a way out so that you can stand up under it" (1 Corinthians 10:13, NIV).

So you can quit making excuses such as, "It was just too strong a temptation." God wouldn't have let it hit you if you couldn't have handled it with His defense tactics. You don't need to constantly make allowances for your old self (Romans 13:14) by saying, "I'm just more prone to sin than other Christians." You can enjoy your role as an *overcomer* (1 John 5:4-5). You can live in the world without becoming *of* it.

But will you fail? Will you take on world-system actions, thoughts, or attitudes sometimes? Will you give in to temptation even though God has provided His defense tactics? Uh-huh. (Read 1 John 1:8, 10.) But the Lord also stuck a confession principle in the Bible just because He expects us to need it: "If we confess our sins, He is faithful and righteous to forgive us our sins and to cleanse us from all unrighteousness" (1 John 1:9).

You'll fail. So will I. But we can grow in our discernment, in figuring out what worldliness is, and in overcoming the temptation to give in to worldliness. We can overcome the world!

II
THE DISCIPLE IN THE WORLD

6 The Disciple and *Self* in the World

"Most of the time I hate myself." The expression on Odessa's face told me she wasn't kidding.

"How come you'd say a dumb thing like that?" I asked.

"Do you know what it's like to be half black?" she replied. "My mother moved with us six kids up to Missouri from Louisiana. We're Creole, so we got flak both from the blacks and the whites.

You just learn to live with it; you get used to the idea that you're worthless to everybody. But I *could* sing. So just before my graduation from high school, we had a music assembly at school. All the white kids sat on one side of the gym and the blacks on the other. That's just the way it was.

"So, anyway, I was going to sing the song 'Summertime' at the assembly. I walked across the gym to ask my voice teacher something. He was white. Then—" Odessa licked her lips. "Then these white guys started throwing wads of paper at us, then somebody threw a book. Then a bunch of black guys came running across the gym and—" She started crying, then stopped. "It went on for about three days. Two people in the town were killed. My voice teacher was fired and told to leave town. I was expelled two weeks before graduation."

"Have you ever gone back?"

"No," she said. "I never finished high school. I don't sing anymore. I'm not the same color as anybody else in the world. I hate myself." She started crying again. "I hate myself."

The Big Little Question

Did you ever hate yourself? Ever look in the mirror and want to throw up? Ever feel as if you wanted to strangle yourself because of something you did wrong? If there's any place to start putting together a lifestyle of discipleship, it's right where you live—in your *self*. Ready to start? On a piece of paper or in your head, answer the question, "Who am I?"

Have a little trouble with that one? Let's try

another brainteaser. On paper or in your brain, jot
down a list of words or phrases that describes you:

I am _____

I am _____

I am _____

I am _____

I am _____

I am _____

I am _____

I am _____

Got a little tough around the seventh or eighth
"I am," right? That's because our culture has trouble with that big little question: "Who am I?" And
since you're in this culture—*in* the world—some
of the world's trouble with that question has probably rubbed off on you. But as a discerning disciple, you can enjoy the out-of-this world privilege
of knowing exactly *who you are* and *what you're
worth*. Really. First, however, let's meet that master of self-confusion, Willy Worldly!

INTERVIEWER: Well, Willy. Today we'd like to pin
down who Willy Worldly really is.

WILLY WORLDLY: Great. I value myself. I find my
identity in what I have and what I do, OK?

INT: OK, Willy, what do you *have* that identifies
you, that makes you valuable as a person?

WW: My possessions show the real me, you know?
I have a 12-string guitar, a skateboard, my own
Mickey Mouse telephone, nine shirts, a Suzuki
dirt bike, two toothbrushes, a set of Harvard Clas-
sics, seven pairs of boxer shorts, four—

INT: Fine, Willy, fine. Tells us much. And what do
you *do*?

WW: I play guitar, ride skateboards, talk on my

Mickey Mouse phone, wear sharp shirts, ride my Suzuki dirt bike—

INT: Fine, Willy, fine. Now we get to the biggie. Who are you?

WW: Not "Who am I?" OK? Just "What am I?" I'm a guy who's generous, who's fun, shrewd, kind, impatient, calm, athletic, organized, ambitious—

INT: Fine, Willy. But those thing just *describe* you. How do you *define* the real Willy Worldly?

WW: Getting tough on me, huh? I guess I'm a descendant of some primeval soup and amino acids. I'm not sure where I'm headed, but ... I'm my mother's son, I'm an all-conference halfback, I'm a stock boy at Crumby's, I'm my grandfather's grandson, I'm—

Tired of listening to Willy? I am. But his answers could be expected from a world-system person. World-system identity and self-worth always revolve around the things you have, the things you do, your attributes, and the roles you play. And the big question is never really answered in the world because "Who I am" is ultimately tied in to "Who God is." And world-system thinking doesn't make that connection.

So how should a disciple answer the big question, "Who am I?" Put on your Spirit-guided wisdom. Let's compare Willy's standards of *identity* and *self-worth* with God's standards.

What You Have

Are you ready for this? Jesus said, "No one of you can be My disciple who does not give up all his own possessions" (Luke 14:33). Jesus' disciples can't take their identity from their possessions because they don't possess anything! One of the keys of being a real disciple is giving up ownership of everything.

Hold on, now. That doesn't mean you're not to *use* anything. Jesus' original disciples wore clothes; Peter lived in a house. But following God's standard does mean that a disciple should think of himself as owning nothing, since God owns everything. David wrote, "Thine, O Lord, is the greatness and the power and the glory and the victory and the majesty, indeed everything that is in the heavens and the earth" (1 Chronicles 29:11).

The things that God lets you use still belong to Him. So your identity and value as a person aren't wrapped up in what you have, or what you own. It's no good thinking: *I'm the kid who has $1,000 in the bank*, or *I'm the girl with the best clothes at school*. A disciple doesn't find identity from these things.

What You Do

Ready for another balloon popper? Not only have you *got* nothing, you can *do* nothing! You can't even live or breathe or move or exist on your own (Acts 17:25-28). Jesus said, "Apart from Me you can do nothing" (John 15:5). The world system says that what you *do* defines you—what job you work at, what sports you play, what activities you're involved in. But God says that what *you* do is zilch apart from His doing it through you.

Remember the first step of the formula for discipleship? Deny self. *Not* to deny the old self results in doing all kinds of things that amount to nothing. The person who under his own power goes to church, pats a sick chicken on the head, and gives a nickel to world missions is really doing nothing. When judged by God's standard, that person's "good works" will simply go up in smoke (1 Corinthians 3:11-15). Only what God has done through him will amount to anything. Doing-it-yourself = nothing. So it's useless for a Christian to determine *who he is* and *what's important about himself* by what he does.

Who You Are: Self-identity

Philosophers have filled hundreds of books trying to answer the big question, "Who am I?" And we're going to try to answer it in just a few paragraphs. So expect to have to think, and expect a simplified shot at answering the big question. Here we go:

• You're a person created in God's image (Genesis 1:26). This means you were designed to be like God in knowledge, righteousness, and holiness of truth! (Colossians 3:10; Ephesians 4:24) You were made to be immortal, to exist forever (1 Corinthians 15:53).

• You're a body, soul, and spirit (1 Thessalonians 5:23). You're a unique being among God's creations. Animals have no spirits; angels have no natural bodies.

Visualize the interaction of your body, soul, and spirit (p. 81 diagram):

• You're designed by God as a one-of-a-kind creation. David realized the incredible privilege

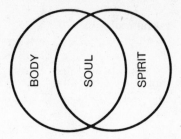

of being formed as a person by God Himself: "For You created my inmost being; You knit me together in my mother's womb. . . . My frame was not hidden from You when I was made in the secret place. When I was woven together in the depths of the earth, Your eyes saw my unformed body. All the days ordained for me were written in Your book before one of them came to be" (Psalm 139:13, 15-16, NIV).

You have a specially designed body, a unique, individual spirit, and a resulting soul unlike any other creature in the universe. It is as if God stopped everything He was doing just to design *you*.

"We are His workmanship" (Ephesians 2:10) is a phrase which literally translates into "we are His *masterpiece*"! Regardless of what the world system thinks, regardless of what a disciple who goes by world-system standards thinks, God says you are His special masterpiece.

● And God knows you personally. Since the first moment of your existence, your name has been written in what the Bible calls the Book of Life. When you were born again spiritually, your name was again written in heaven—this time in the

Lamb's Book of Life (Revelation 13:8; 21:27). You're on a first-name basis with God. He knows you personally, thoroughly. He even knows the number of hairs on your noggin (Matthew 10:30). You're not just a digit/decimal/binary number. Science may view you as an insignificant product of the evolutionary process, but God sees you quite differently. You're special, exceptional, personal to God.

So let's put it together. Who are you?

You're a special person created in God's image.

You're a body-soul-spirit being, unique among God's creations.

You're God's one-of-a-kind design—His masterpiece.

You're known intimately by Him.

You're made to be God-like, to exist forever!

Now read that list about four times, substituting "I'm" for "you're." Forget the world-system idea that you're just an evolutionary speck on a tiny mudball spinning through megaspace. Catch a goose-bump glimpse of who you really are!

What You Are Worth: Self-esteem

What's good about you? What's impressive or important about you? Try this checklist:

_____ I'm really good-looking.

_____ Everybody envies my hair.

_____ I'm smart.

_____ I'm athletic, coordinated.

_____ My body is shaped perfectly.

_____ I'm talented.

_____ I'm creative, witty.

_____ I'm sexy.

_____ I'm a leader.

_____ My voice sounds mature and sophisticated.

How'd you score? 5 out of 10? 2 out of 10? 10 out of 10? −3 out of 10? Well, don't panic if you flunked. Because *none* of these items have a thing to do with your value as a person. That checklist comes straight out of the Pit via the world system.

Remember, in the world system, self-importance comes from what you have and do. Notice during the next few days how many people try to impress you with lines such as:

- Man, you should see all the trophies I've got at home.
- I've got the fastest wheels in town.
- I've got the inside story on . . .
- My uncle's neighbor's kid's friend is a movie star.
- I've been to Hawaii so many times it's boring.
- I've got all kinds of money.
- I've done it all.

But besides what you have or do, the world gauges self-worth in three big areas: *appearance*, *intelligence*, and *talent*. I don't need to argue the point. You know that the girl with the "Perfect 10" face and body will be chosen for Asparagus Queen long before the plain-faced contestants. The smart guy will probably get a better job than the slower thinker. The macho halfback will get more attention than the 98-pound weakling. You know all that. You live with it.

These false standards of self-worth have a firm hold on the world's way of thinking. They're powerful. But they're also frustrating—frustrating first because, sooner or later, there's always a new kid in town who's better looking, smarter, or more talented. So when the newest phenomenon shows up, the world-system rating scale has to be adjusted. And suddenly nobody's worth what he used to be. (Cheryl is the prettiest girl in her small high school. Then she goes to college where hundreds of girls are fashion-model material. So now Cheryl's not so special anymore, not so noticed, not so important.) Comparison is the law of the world-system jungle, and comparison is frustrating.

Another reason that a standard of beauty, brains, and ability is frustrating is that these goodies always fade. The woman who was once important because of her looks begins to wrinkle. The whiz-kid who stunned the world with his intellectual pizzazz gets senile. The football hero grows fat and slow. And every person who judges himself by world-system standards must one day feel his self-worth crumble.

What He Thinks about You

Let's probe just a little deeper into this matter of what makes you important. Think through the following questions and find out what God has to say in the Bible about your worth:

1. Even though the world system bases self-worth on appearance, the real value of a person is found by looking at what? (See 1 Samuel 16:7.)

2. How important is physical strength? (See Psalm 147:10-11.)
3. How valuable is intelligence? (See 1 Corinthians 1:26-27.)
4. How will a disciple who rates low on the world's scale feel as he takes on God's ideas about his value? (See 2 Corinthians 12:10.)
5. If a disciple is good-looking, smart, or talented, how much importance should be placed on these things? (See Philippians 3:4-8.)
6. Good looks, intelligence, or talent might be part of God's design for you. If so, how should you use these qualities? (See Colossians 3:17.)
7. True or false:
   —It's wrong to be smart.
   —God loves you because of your talent.
   —Good looks can be used by God.
   —God can use weakness.
   —Plain looks are bad.
   —Talented Christians are more important than non-talented ones.
   —It's OK to be handsome, plain, smart, uncoordinated, talented, a slow learner, weak, or strong.

It's clear that your value as a person isn't determined by what you have or what you do or how you look or how brainy or talented you are. Right? So what are you left with? Why are you important?

You're valuable because God made you. And as the old phrase goes, "God don't make no junk."

If you were in an accident that left you paralyzed and in a coma, you wouldn't be worth much to the world. You might not look too good. You couldn't do much thinking. And you'd be unable to perform the teeniest task. But you'd still be a "10" on God's scale. He'd still love you, think about you, guard you, bless you. He'd still want you. You'd always be incredibly important to Him— just as you are right now—because He made you.

Love It!

Maybe you're feeling that all this talk about *self* is very unspiritual, very selfish. But that depends on which self you're talking about. Use your discernment as you consider hating your old self but loving your new self.

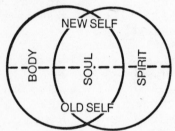

Old-self thinking is selfish. Disciples are to lay "aside the old self with its evil practices" (Colossians 3:9). But thinking about yourself as a whole new person isn't selfish at all. In fact, the Apostle Paul commanded: "Do not think of yourself more highly than you ought, but rather *think of yourself with sober judgment*" (Romans 12:3, NIV, italics mine).

Loving the old self is selfish. But disciples are commanded to love their neighbors as they love themselves (Luke 10:27). You have to love yourself properly before you can love others properly. So go ahead, love your new self. It's OK. You're worth it.

How do you properly love yourself? "And this is love, that we walk according to His commandments" (2 John 6). You love yourself properly by taking on God's standards of self-identity and self-worth. Reprogram your world-tainted self-concepts with the truth about who you are and why you're important:

I'm a special person created in God's image.

I'm a body-soul-spirit being, unique among God's creations.

I'm God's one-of-a-kind design—His masterpiece.

I'm known intimately by Him.

I'm made to be God-like, to exist forever!

I'm valuable because God made me!

7
The Disciple and Thinking in the World

"Life is crazy, so do whatever. Just don't hurt anybody else, understand?"

—*Existential Edna*

"Man is the measure. Given enough time, man can solve any problem, do anything."

—*Huey Humanist*

"There are absolutely no absolutes."

—*Rosanna Relativist*

"If it works, it's right. Right?"
—Pratney Pragmatist
*"Hey, all I really know is what's happened to
me. All I really know is what I read in the papers."*
—Eudalfo Empiricist
*"If it feels good, do it. If it feels good, do it. If
it . . ."*
—Harry Hedonist
*"Pure brainpower. I can figure life out by fig-
uring it out. Easy."*
—Rodney Rationalist
*"My thoughts are not your thoughts, neither
are your ways My ways."*
—God (Isaiah 55:8)

Mind Games

God's thoughts are different from the world's
thoughts. In fact, they are so different that God's
ideas often seem foolish to people in the world
(1 Corinthians 1:18), and the world's wisdom often
seems foolish to God (1 Corinthians 1:19-20).

That doesn't mean that everything non-Christians think up is stupid and sinful. Far from it.
Unbelievers come up with brilliant theories and
valuable insights. But worldly thinking is foolish
when it leaves God out (Psalm 14:1). "Huey Humanist," "Rosanna Relativist," "Harry Hedonist,"
and the others are foolish because their ideas about
life ignore God. They're the types who are "always learning and never able to come to the
knowledge of the truth" (2 Timothy 3:7). In God's
eyes, their thinking is ignorant (Ephesians 4:18),

bigheaded (Colossians 2:18), and blind (2 Corinthians 4:14).

But even Christians can slip into the world's "leave-God-out" way of thinking. For example, it's easy enough to think, "Today or tomorrow, we shall go to such and such a city, and spend a year there and engage in business and make a profit" (James 4:13). Nothing wrong with such a plan, except one thing—it leaves God out. So James reminded us, "You do not know what your life will be like tomorrow. You are just a vapor that appears for a little while and then vanishes away. . . . You ought to say, 'If the Lord wills, we shall live and also do this or that' " (James 4:14-15).

So, thinking that ignores God can sometimes seem quite harmless. It takes wisdom to know what kind of thinking is worldly and what kind isn't. The disciple who intends to be *in* the world but not *of* it has to be careful about how he thinks. The reason: "As [a person] thinks within himself, so he is" (Proverbs 23:7). You become what you think.

The hard part about developing a Christian mind is that we disciples live "in the midst of a crooked and perverse generation" (Philippians 2:15). The whole world pressures us to think worldly. TV, radio, books, music, magazines, and especially people around us are constantly urging, "Think the same way we think. Conform."

Surrounded by all these pressures, the disciple has to practice *discernment*. He has to use Spirit-controlled *wisdom* and *ability* to filter out world-style thinking. As Martin Luther said, "You cannot stop the birds from flying over your head, but you can stop them from nesting in your hair."

Truth or Consequences

As I boarded a flight from Dallas to New Orleans, I sat down next to an elderly man. "Hi", I said as I buckled in.

"Will we crash?" the man replied.

"I don't think so." I noticed he'd pulled his safety belt so tightly he could hardly breathe.

"It happens, you know," he mumbled as the stewardess went into her pitch about safety devices and emergency procedures. Halfway through her talk, the old man noticed I was reading. "Pay attention!" he demanded, reaching over and closing my book.

I didn't read much during the rest of the flight either, thanks to my jittery fellow passenger. He kept asking questions: "What's that noise?" "What's happening to the engine?" "Why aren't the other passengers concerned?" He told me this wasn't his first flight, so I couldn't figure out why he was acting so weird. Finally we touched down in New Orleans. The man was so relieved, I thought he was going to cry.

"We made it," he gasped. "After all those problems with DC-10s and the crash of that DC-10. And *we* made it!"

"This isn't a DC-10. It's a Boeing 727."

"Not a DC-10!" His eyes bulged. His face turned beet red. "I thought this was a DC-10! A man at the Dallas airport *told* me this was a DC-10! I wouldn't have—of course I wouldn't have acted so foolishly if I'd known! I—I—"

He had made the flight miserable for both of us because he had acted on false information. Likewise, a disciple can mess up his life if he believes the false information of the world—if he doesn't learn to screen out world-system thinking.

Garbage in, Garbage Out

The working motto of computer programming is "GIGO": "Garbage in—garbage out." Whatever gets fed into the memory banks of a computer will eventually come sputtering back out. The Apostle Paul didn't know computers, but he knew about "GIGO." Paul wrote: "The one who sows to his own flesh shall from the flesh reap corruption, but the one who sows to the Spirit shall from the Spirit reap eternal life" (Galatians 6:8). If you stuff your head with info from the fleshly old self, then fleshly, old-self living is what will come out of you.

Think of it this way: Your computer-brain receives knowledge as input. Output from that knowledge is displayed in the actions and attitudes of your lifestyle. If you program your mind with the garbage thinking of the world, one day your life is going to smell like the city dump. If you program your mind with God's thinking, your lifestyle is going to reflect Christlike qualities.

Reprogramming

So far, we've focused on the need to screen out world-system thinking. But there's also a positive side to having a Christian mind. The Christian whose brain has been programmed by the world system—and that includes almost every disciple—needs to reprogram his mind with God's thoughts. The mind needs to be renewed:

"Be *renewed* in the spirit of your mind" (Ephesians 4:23). "Put on the new self who is being *renewed* to a true knowledge" (Colossians 3:10). "Be transformed by the *renewing* of your mind" (Romans 12:2, italics mine). And how are our minds renewed? We're programmed as we open our minds to God's Word. The true info about life is found in the "milk" and "meat" of the Bible.

I was guiding a Bible study called "How to Be Hungry." We began by working through a section in 1 Peter: "Putting aside all malice and all guile and hypocrisy and envy and all slander, like newborn babes, long for the pure milk of the Word . . ." (1 Peter 2:1-2).

I explained to the group, "As you peel away those world-system attitudes, you'll uncover a *desire*, a hunger for God's thoughts in the Word."

"But it doesn't *do* anything. I don't feel any different if I study the Bible or not," said Karen.

"I know what you mean," one of the guys said. "But whatever you *feel*, God promises you'll grow. See, in verse 2—'that by it you may grow.' "

"Right," I said. "Then as you get more accustomed to thinking God's thoughts, you can start chewing on the meat of the Word—the heavies." Then I read: "Everyone who partakes only of milk is not accustomed to the Word of righteousness, for he is a babe. But solid food is for the mature" (Hebrews 5:13-14).

"So what?" somebody said.

Karen answered, "I'm not exactly sure what that verse means. But I know I'd like to be able to understand how God thinks about a situation before I pray about it. I'd like to be sharing God's thoughts when I tell someone about how to be a disciple. When I read a part of the Bible, I'd like to have a better background in the whole Bible, so I could understand better. I'd like to be tuned in to God's way of thinking when I fellowship with other Christians."

"So how do you get God's thoughts to be your thoughts?" I asked.

"Read," said one of our more brilliant guys. "The old Bible teacher, G. Campbell Morgan, said that the Bible comes alive when you follow three rules: read, read, and then read some more."

"No, you've got to study," said somebody else. "You can't just run over the words. You've got to slow down and ask what's being said—and why—and what does it mean—and what am I going to do about it? Stuff like that. But studying is the key."

"Nope. It's meditation on the Word," another kid said. "Read, analyze, visualize, or picture in your mind what's being said. Then memorize it. That way you make God's Word a part of you. You make His thoughts your thoughts."

"So what do you think, Stearns?" came the question.

"All of the above," I replied.

Reading, studying, and meditating on God's Word will reprogram, it will renew, the mind. Getting into the Bible will get the garbage out and put the good stuff in.

The Well-Fed Disciple

Warning: There's a three-headed monster that'll try to keep you from feeding your brain with God's way of thinking. The three heads are:

- **The lust of the flesh.** Your physical desire to sleep will try to keep you from learning God's thoughts. Your physical desire to go swimming on a hot day, to go out and jog, to eat, to be lazy, will try to short-circuit your reprogramming process.

- **The lust of the eyes.** Especially if you're living around non-Christians or worldly Christians, your ego will try to keep you from getting into God's thoughts. The Enemy will tell you that people will think you're weird if you read your Bible.

- **The pride of life.** There's a little inner voice that says, "Hey, I ain't a bad kid. I'm a Christian. I'm living a respectable Christian life. I pray. I go to church where people tell me about God. What do I need to get into God's Word for anyhow? Maybe He'll tell me something I don't want to know!"

The three-headed monster is that familiar old character called—you guessed it—worldliness. Remember what to do when tempted by the world system.

- **Use the "flee tactic."** Physically, get up and *move* to a position where you can read/ study/meditate on the Bible.

- **Rebel against peer pressure**. Decide to pick up on God's thoughts instead of other people's thoughts.

- **Ask God to rebuke Satan.**

And forget the fact that learning God's thoughts

might not have been one of your stronger habits: "Forgetting what lies behind and reaching forward to what lies ahead, I press on toward the goal for the prize of the upward call of God in Christ Jesus" (Philippians 3:13-14).

8
The Disciple and Money in the World

The screen is a blank, fuzzy gray. Suddenly a deep voice booms, "And now—it's time for the Money Game!" TV cameras pan the screaming crowd. People are grinning, clapping, glancing nervously at the camera. The announcer speaks again: "And here's our Money Game host—Monty Dazzle!" The crowd goes wild. Two ladies in the audience lose their cool and leap up to dance in the aisle.

Monty Dazzle bounces out from behind velvet curtains as the band blares.

"Thank you, thank you," Monty says breathlessly. "Thank you, thank you. Well, folks, welcome to another round of the Money Game. Our contestants today are . . ." The cameras cut to three faces grinning behind a long desk. "Willy Worldy! Claude Cultural Christian! And Dicky Disciple!" The crowd explodes again. The two ladies do the rhumba.

Monty's grin locks into place as he says, "And the first question is, 'Why money?' I'll read that again. Audience, you be formulating your own answers. Again, 'Why Money?' "

The bass in the band *bip-dums* background jive while the contestants prepare their answers. Finally Willy Worldly taps his buzzer. "Money," Willy grins, "brings the possibility of all kinds of"—he rolls his eyes—"sensual pleasures. You're looked up to. And with enough money you can do whatever you want, be your own boss, not have to take grief from anybody, have power, rule the world—"

"How about that?" screams Monty Dazzle. The crowd yells and whistles. Claude Cultural Christian's buzzer goes off. "Your answer, Claude?" Monty says.

"No," sighs Claude. "Money is a necessary evil. It's very religious not to have any. On the other hand, without money, what ministry would there be? I mean, God really needs your contributions for His work. Otherwise He's up a creek, so to speak. I'll mention my address at the end of this broadcast, and if you'll send a gift of more than $25, I will send you, absolutely free, my autographed picture which will prove to Saint Peter as you enter those—" Claude stares enraptured at the ceiling, *"pearly gates.* I say, it will prove to Saint Peter that you have truly done your duty as—"

"How about that?" screams Monty Dazzle. The crowd doesn't yell quite as loudly this time, but the two dancing ladies again leap out into the aisle. The crowd simmers down. Monty wipes the sweat off his forehead. "Well, Dicky. Your response?"

Dick Disciple says, "Money is . . . money is like a jump rope."

"How about that?" screams Monty Dazzle. The crowd yawns. The two ladies sit and scratch. "He has such wit," screams Monty into the silence. "What wit, eh?" Then he slides over to the announcer. "Where'd we get *him*?" Monty whispers. "He's off in his own little world, huh? He sure doesn't belong to *this* one."

Ownership

And now, folks—it's time for—discovering what discipleship has to do with money and possessions! Knowing that the world system's view of money is uncertain (1 Timothy 6:17), deceitful (Matthew 13:22), and corrupted (James 5:1-6), let's get the lowdown on loot.

How does society view material things?

- Capitalism says the individual owns them.
- Communism says the state owns them.
- Christianity says God owns them. All of them.

Remember the chapter about the disciple and

self? It hit on the fact that people own zilch, that God is the owner of everything. God is the supplier of all possessions (1 Timothy 6:17). Every good thing comes from Him as His gift (Ecclesiastes 5:19; James 1:17). And the Apostle Paul reminds us disciples that not even our chubby-cheeked bodies belong to us. They're God's too (1 Corinthians 6:19-20). "The earth is the Lord's, and all it contains" (Psalm 24:1).

Now, make a quick mental list of the things you "own." Include everything you can think of, from clothes to money to record albums to tennis rackets. And remember this: Every cotton pickin' thing that you call yours is really God's!

What difference does it make to recognize God's ownership? First, knowing who owns the stuff you've got means you answer to Him for the way you take care of it. I watched a guy putting away a guitar at a retreat one weekend. He handled the thing like it was a newborn baby. He polished it first, wrapped it carefully in a cloth bag, eased it into the guitar case, and checked the latches before picking up the case. "Hey," I commented, "you really take care of that thing."

"Oh, it's not mine," he said. "It's my brother's. He just let me bring it along this weekend, so I've got to be careful with it."

Get it? Knowing that God owns "your" things should prompt you to hang up your tuxedo instead of stuffing it under your bed. To change the oil in your car more often than every other year. To make sure your prize houseplant doesn't die of thirst.

Something else happens when you recognize God's ownership. Committing what you have to

Him enables God to use "your" money and possessions to teach you a lot of good stuff.

The day I bought a van, I told the Lord, "It's Yours." I drove it to a snow camp near Lake Tahoe and "suffered for the Lord" through two days of snow skiing. I also talked with the snow campers about committing their money and possessions to God. So, naturally, as I leaped into the van to head for home, I dropped the clutch. As I watched the other vehicles drive away, I simply reminded the Lord that this problem was now His. The clutch of His van was kaput and I hoped He'd let me know what He intended to do about it.

What He did was arrange for me to enjoy two more days at the snow camp. I learned some good stuff as I studied His Word during those quiet days.Then He arranged for the tow truck that came from Reno to be driven by a couple who asked me, "What are your religious beliefs?" I had a captive audience as I talked about Christ all the way to the repair shop in Reno.

God used His possession—the van—to arrange my schedule, my activities, and my contacts with people. And the whole time I could enjoy whatever He had me doing because the problem wasn't mine. The van wasn't mine.

Ownership problems? Some people, Christians included, refuse to recognize God's ownership. They'd like to believe that they own the things God's allowed them to use. These people set themselves up for a couple of nasty problems.

First, the person who insists on claiming exclusive ownership rights can't live a lifestyle of discipleship. You can't live like a real disciple while you're clinging to your right to own things (Luke 14:33).

Second, whoever convinces himself that *he* owns the things around him gets fooled into thinking he doesn't need God. The *things* that fill his life camouflage his real needs. He develops the kind of attitude which the church at Laodicea had: "You say 'I am rich, and have become wealthy, and have need of nothing,' and you do not know that you are wretched and miserable and poor and blind and naked" (Revelation 3:17).

Imagine a young dude strutting away from his Mercedes, frowning because his valet is taking too long preparing his afternoon snack of caviar. Imagine this rich guy smiling as his maids pamper him beside his pool, then burping and saying, "Who is the Lord?" (Proverbs 30:8-9)

People often stuff the spiritually empty spot inside them with their "possessions," everything from mag wheels to designer jeans. Pretending to own things disguises their need for God.

Giving up. How might your life change if you really gave everything you own back to God? Why don't you find out? Remember that mental list you supposedly thought up a few pages back? Now grab some paper and list the items you "own."

Next, carefully go over the list and say out loud that God is the owner of each item. You should probably do this in a secluded spot. Otherwise, somebody might send for the men in the white coats if you sit at Taco Bell mumbling: "God, You own my Oakland Raiders jersey. God, You own the 43¢ in my pocket. You own the Etch-a-Sketch Uncle Sig gave me seven years ago. . . ."

"No one of you can be My disciple who does

not give up all his own possessions" (Luke 14:33).
All kinds of cults misuse this verse to persuade
people to leave home, to throw away every material thing they have. If that's what Christ really
meant, true disciples would have to be jailed for
indecent exposure! The words *give up* in this verse
mean "bid good-bye to." And that's just the action
you've taken if you worked through the ownership
list. You said "good-bye" to your claim of ownership on everything you have.

So now what?

Stewardship

If you don't own anything, what do you do about
the stuff you thought you owned? You use it. Or
abuse it.

For example, suppose you and I decide to switch
houses for our vacations. I come to stay in your
house for three weeks, and you come to stay in
my home in beautiful downtown Prairie Grove,
Arkansas.

The three weeks go by. You use my house to
live in, eat in, sleep in. You leave it clean as a
whistle and head for home. OK so far? You've
properly used my possessions.

Then you arrive at your place and climb through
the four-foot-high grass to reach the front door.
Two signs have been tacked on the doorpost:
"Daisy's Day-care: Upstairs" and "ROLLER
DERBY EVERY FRIDAY NIGHT!" I meet you
just inside.

"Listen, Stearns—" you sputter.

"If it's about the garbage, don't panic. The health

department promised not to condemn the place till you got home. I just forgot to put out the trash, and you know how it collects. You'll find it all in the hallway closet."

"But—-"

I'm all smiles as I tell you, "The downstairs worked great for Friday night Roller Derby! Some house you got here. Want some fried baloney?"

You stumble to the kitchen and glance out the back door as 14 screaming four-year-olds cascade down the stairs. "I—I—"

"Oh, the backyard," I say. "Started to dig you a swimming hole, but I pooped out about halfway through; so I just made it into one fine mud pit. I'm raisin' you five Arkansas razorback hogs back there. See 'em?"

"Those little kids—"

"Daisy's Day-care upstairs." The doorbell rings. "Oh, must be some early-comers for the Roller Derby tonight! Excuse me."

"The grass —" you mumble.

"Not to worry," I smile over my shoulder. "Makes great fun for wild boar hunts when one of them razorbacks breaks out of the backyard. Great fun."

Get the point? You can misuse somebody else's possessions.

The way you use or misuse God's possessions is called "stewardship." Just as a steward who's hired to manage a mansion or an estate takes care of things and people that aren't his, a disciple is to use God's possessions properly, as a trustworthy and faithful steward (1 Corinthians 4:2). As a steward or manager of whatever God gives you to use, remember:

- God's kingdom always comes first in your attitude toward things and how you use them (Matthew 6:33).
- Diligence and discipline are musts in stewardship (Luke 16:10-12).
- Your use of the things God trusts you with is a vital part of your relationship with Him (Matthew 25:21).

So how do you properly handle the things God lets you use? Maybe the best way to see how to handle God's possessions is to focus on that slippery substance called *money*.

Making Money

God gives you the ability to make money: "Remember the Lord your God, for it is He who is giving you power to make wealth" (Deuteronomy 8:18). Surprised? Maybe you've been programmed to think that God expects every disciple to be poor, that money is the root of all evil. Nope, "The *love* of money is a root of all sorts of evil" (1 Timothy 6:10, italics mine). It's OK to make money. God gives you the ability to do that.

Adam was placed in the garden "to cultivate it and keep it" (Genesis 2:15). Likewise, God's plan is for you to work hard (Romans 12:11) and invest (Matthew 25:14-27). Not for you to get rich quick (Proverbs 28:22). Not for you to wait for pennies to drop out of the sky as did the clod in King Solomon's proverbs (Proverbs 26:14-15). So go ahead and take the opportunities God gives you to acquire money and things. Work (Ephesians 4:28). But watch your motives.

"Those who want to get rich fall into temptation and a snare and many foolish and harmful desires which plunge men into ruin and destruction. For the love of money is a root of all sorts of evil, and some by longing for it have wandered away from the faith, and pierced themselves with many a pang" (1 Timothy 6:9-10). If you want to make money to fulfill misdirected physical desires, or to look good, or to make you free from dependence on God, look out. The world system's money game has you by the throat.

Saving Money

Plan ahead in your management of God's money. Keep your brain in gear on money matters: "Know well the condition of your flocks, and pay attention to your herds" (Proverbs 27:23). Figure out when your wardrobe will need replacements, when your car will need front-end alignment, and save toward those needs. Be like an ant, "which prepares her food in the summer, and gathers her provision in the harvest" (Proverbs 6:8). Don't think it's unspiritual to look ahead within the will of God. Remember that "the plans of the diligent lead surely to advantage" (Proverbs 21:5).

But in all your planning, budgeting, and saving, remember what you're doing. You're just taking care of some things that don't belong to you. Beware of getting stuck on all that dough you're saving. Don't think of your savings as *your* treasure. "Where your treasure is, there will your heart be also" (Matthew 6:21).

Your real treasure is in heaven (Matthew 6:20).

So don't think you've got any treasure on earth just because you're wisely saving some of God's wealth.

Spending Money

This category is the sparsest one in this "how-to-use-God's money" section. The Bible really doesn't say much about spending money, though spending seems to be the real whoop-de-do in the world-system money game.

But here's one biblical principle to chew on: "Have you found honey? Eat only what you need, lest you have it in excess and vomit it" (Proverbs 25:16). Nice verse, huh? It vividly points out the disciple's rule of thumb for spending God's bucks: Use some of God's money to take care of your *needs* and the needs of your family, if you're supporting one (1 Timothy 5:8).

Don't go off on a big guilt trip on this point. Just be sure to talk over your purchases with God. After all, it's His money you're spending.

Giving Money

The new preacher thundered from the pulpit, "We as a church are going to get up and walk forward!"

"Amen," the old deacon shouted. "Let the church walk!"

"And then," said the preacher, "this church is going to run!"

"Amen, preacher. Let the church run!"

"Then! Then the church is going to fly!"

"Whew! Amen, brother! Let the church fly!"

"Now, you know," the preacher said, "that in order to fly, the church is going to need money."

"Let the church walk," stated the old deacon. "Let it walk."

If you're like that deacon, or a good many church members, you've probably heard enough about giving money. But let's break away from the world-system and cultural-Christian ideas about giving. It's discernment time.

Did you ever see an old TV series rerun called "The Millionaire"? This guy knocked on people's doors and presented them with checks for a million bucks. Then the plot would show how each newly rich person's life was bettered or worsened or whatever. Well, put yourself behind the door when that guy knocks.

"Hello, my name is Michael B. Anthony. And I have here a check made out to you for $1 million."

After you pull his hair to make sure he's not your neighbor in a wig trying to make a fool out of you, you take the check. What'll you do with it? Save some? Sure. Spend some? Sure. Give some away? Sure—but how?

Heard of tithing? "Tithe" means a tenth, and lots of Christians think that 90 percent of their money and possessions belongs to them and 10 percent belongs to God. So you could tithe. You could run down to the church, dump off a cool $100,000 of your new wealth, and skip off to spend the other $900,000 as you please!

But are you remembering that everything—the whole million—belongs to God in the first place? Ten percent isn't His share; He owns 100 percent!

If you believe in always setting aside a tenth of

your income for God, fine. That's a good way to
be disciplined in your giving. But don't get the
attitude that 90 percent is yours and 10 percent is
God's. That you give because you *have* to, or that
10 percent is all you're supposed to give. Instead,
center your giving around these New Testament
principles:

- **Give regularly** (1 Corinthians 16:2).
- **Make your giving a personal thing between
you and God** (Matthew 6:4).The urge to announce
how much you give is just an attack of world-system ego.
- **Give to people in need** (Ephesians 4:28;
1 John 3:17; Acts 20:35).
- **Discipline yourself to give** (2 Corinthians
9:7a).
- **Be sincere about giving voluntarily**
(2 Corinthians 9:7). A grudging, duty-bound attitude in giving stinks. Compare Israel's stinky sac-
rifices, given when their hearts were miles from
God (Isaiah 1:11-13), with the Philippians' whole-
hearted giving that was "a fragrant aroma, an ac-
ceptable sacrifice, well-pleasing to God"
(Philippians 4:18).
- **Get in on the fun of giving.** Give cheerfully
(2 Corinthians 9:7). A "cheerful giver" is literally
a "hilarious giver"!
- **Realize that by giving earthly money, you're
adding to your real treasure in heaven** (Philippians 4:17). Paul wanted the Philippians to give,
not for the sake of giving, but for the profit in-
creasing in their heavenly account.

So with those guidelines you'd know what to do
with your million bucks, right? You'd *discern* how

much and to whom and when and how to give. Of course "The Millionaire" was just a fake TV show. You probably don't have $1 million in your pocket.

But why not use the same giving guidelines for the money and possessions you do have? Learn to give from what God gives you. Don't give to pay Him off or give Him His percentage. It's already all His. Get out of the rut that says God needs your money. Realize He wants you to practice giving for the qualities it'll bring into your life—qualities like thankfulness, discipline, trust, sensitivity to others, sincerity, joy.

Money Is like a Jump Rope

Wondered about that statement, didn't you? How is money like a jump rope? Money's like a jump rope because God gives it to us to get us into shape.

Let's say I give one of my daughters two bucks so she can set up a lemonade stand. I don't give her the money so I can beg her to give me 20¢ back. I don't give it to her because I need the money. I give it to her because I know that the thought and planning and work and fun of using the two dollars for a lemonade stand will help her grow. It's a gift that'll help her grow in wisdom, in responsibility, in discipline, and in confidence.

God is certainly a wiser Father than I am. I say this respectfully: He's no dummy to let us use His things, His money. It's all an important part of shaping us up as His disciples.

9
The Disciple and Morality in the World

"What is moral is what you feel good after, and what is immoral is what you feel bad after."
—Hemingway in Death in the Afternoon

"My rackets are run on strictly American lines and they're going to stay that way."
—Al Capone in a 1929 interview

"What is good? All that elevates the feeling of

power, the will to power, the power itself in man.
What is bad? All that proceeds from weakness."
          —*Friedrich Nietzsche in* The AntiChrist
    "All this ethical theory would be great if I didn't
have to figure out how to settle a neighborhood
dispute over someone throwing tomatoes into Mrs.
Hughes' chimney."

                                —*Bill Stearns in*
             Anybody Here Know Right From Wrong?

I'll never forget the bizarre problem of a new
Christian in Oregon. He had been up to his neck
in dope-dealing when he received Christ. So his
problem was: "Is it *right* to pay my junkie the
$600 I still owe him when I know he'll just buy
more heroin with it? What's the right thing to do?"

Morality. Right and wrong. A hefty investigation
of this subject is sort of like trying to pet a por-
cupine. So I won't deal here with the *theory* of
morality and ethics. For theory, read my book
Anybody Here Know Right From Wrong? (a
SonPower Elective) This time around let's talk
about morality in terms of lifestyle—*doing* right
or wrong.

As a disciple, you've got your choice of three
different perspectives on morality. And the first
two don't count.

The *Give-Up* Approach

This is the do-what-is-right-in-your-own-eyes approach to morality. In other words, forget about
all standards. "If it feels good, do it." The thinking
behind the Give-Up approach is: If there's no God

running the universe, why pretend there are rights and wrongs? Why not just do what comes naturally and see what happens?

The Give-Up attitude reminds me of the first time I went sailing. The *Cal 20* was leaping from swell to swell. We'd just loosed the spinnaker sail when I mumbled to the boat's captain, "I'm feeling a little green. What do I do if I get seasick?" "Don't worry," he grinned. "You'll do it." Fans of the Give-Up approach to morality have the same idea: "Don't worry about it. Just do what comes natural."

I don't have to wax eloquent on what world-system immorality looks like. It's an easy approach to recognize, mainly by its spiritual deadness. Paul told the Ephesian disciples that before they received Christ, they were "dead in trespasses and sins" (Ephesians 2:1). So Ichabod Immoral, doing what "comes natural" in a sinful world system, is like a relaxed, dead fish floating downstream. Decisions are easy. The gate is wide and the road is broad. Right and wrong are whatever Icky chooses. And since "all the ways of a man are clean in his own sight" (Proverbs 16:2), Ichabod feels OK about taking this path of least resistance.

Give-Up Problems

But giving up on morality is not without its problems. One problem is that doing whatever you choose may be doing what somebody else doesn't choose. For instance, I lived in a barn with a guy named Ned while I was going to college. Ned and

I found we had very different ideas of what life-in-the-barn should be like. He didn't like the way I came straight home from my part-time job at a meat-packing plant smelling like pickled hog juice. Numb to the fragrance, I didn't think I was doing anything bad at all.

But I was keenly aware of Ned's nasty habit: lying back on his bunk with a .22 and blasting away at the rats that peeked through the holes in the ceiling. It got a little hard to study. I never knew when to expect the next round of fire.

Now, whether or not to shoot rats while your roommate's studying may not be a heavy moral issue. But the point is, doing what I wanted wasn't what Ned wanted, and vice versa. In the same way, when you get into heavy moral questions (Is it right to drink? Is it right to cheat on an exam? Is it right to have an abortion?) everyone has his own idea of what is right or wrong. So your do-whatever routine is bound to collide with some-body else's do-whatever routine. And collisions hurt.

Another problem with this well-traveled life-style is its destination. It leads gradually but ul-timately to destruction (Matthew 7:13)—which is no fun. David wrote that those who live in im-morality are "like the chaff which the wind drives away. . . . the way of the wicked will perish" (Psalm 1:4, 6). The word *perish* in this verse carries the idea of "amounting to zero." A life without moral standards won't amount to anything of lasting value.

When my father-in-law Ralph was a young man, some guys invited him to go out with them one night and whoop it up. Though he wasn't a Chris-

tian at that time, Ralph had reservations about some
of the things that were happening that night. For
instance, he didn't drink as the rest of the guys
guzzled and chugged and guzzled some more.
Finally, the group decided to raise a little havoc
in the local cemetery. But as they stumbled out of
the car, the booze hit home. The whole group
started to vomit and to pass out among the
gravestones.

Ralph still remembers watching that scene from
the car and asking himself, "This is whooping it
up?" In the long run, an immoral lifestyle isn't
pretty.

Give-Up Saints

Even Christians sometimes adopt a Give-Up approach to morality. They give in to the *other-side-
of-the-fence syndrome*, the feeling that the grass
is greener, the living a little more fun, on the world-
system side of the fence. They give up on God's
morality, and live flat-out as part of the world
system.

Ever feel the pull of the *other-side-of-the-fence
syndrome*? Tammy felt it, and decided to climb
the fence. She rebelled against anything and anybody that reminded her of God's principles. She
left home after telling off her parents and insulting
her Christian friends—cutting all the ties she could
with her lifestyle of discipleship. She learned about
sex, about coping with life on drugs, and about
being used by people. And she learned about
being hurt to the heart, about jail cells, and guilt
and hate and abortions.

"What do you really want out of all this?" I asked Tammy one day.

She started to cry. "I want to go home," she said.

"You mean go back to your folks?"

"No. I want to go home," she tapped her chest, "inside."

God doesn't want you to give up on morality and just "go for it." Not because He doesn't want you to have fun, but because He loves you. His lifestyle is best.

When one of my daughters, Erin, was about two, she had visions of being a lumberjack. She loved to climb trees. Every chance she got she climbed up an old elm in our backyard. There was a little tree house up there that looked fun. The climbing down part of her lumberjack routine is what I didn't like. She dropped—like a hunk of lead.

Since I didn't want Erin to be known all her life as "the girl with the flat nose," I wouldn't let her climb to the tree house. Because I loved her, I gave her one of my nobler guidelines: "You get outta that tree!" If she decided to disobey, I disciplined her—because I loved her.

God's discipline of a Christian who gives up on His guidelines of right and wrong is also prompted by His love (Hebrews 12:5-11). But even loving discipline isn't much fun. Ask Erin. So don't bother giving up on morality, OK?

The *Gear-Up* Approach

This is the approach to morality which accepts God's principles of right and wrong, and then tries to live up to them in merely human strength.

This is an alright approach if you just love to do futile things, like trying to shave your tongue. The idea is for natural man—stuck in his old sin nature—to try gearing up to God's supernatural standards of morality.

On a human level, world-system morality is respectable. Even non-Christians can appear to be nicely moral on a human scale. The rich young ruler (Matthew 19:16-22) was undoubtedly one clean man. Not a disciple, he had done all the right things from a human viewpoint. Some of the most morally straight people I know aren't Christians. Some are members of strange cults. Some are atheists.

People of the world system can shape up their behavior to look good because even the old sinful nature has a certain self-discipline. Old-nature discipline *can* change outward behavior. Anybody can vow: "I will never pig out on more than three bean-and-garlic burritos at a time," and stick to that standard by sheer self-discipline.

Gear-Up Problems

Unfortunately, this approach has its problems too. "Why . . . do you submit to [the world's] rules: 'Do not handle! Do not taste! Do not touch!'? Such regulations indeed have an appearance of wisdom, with their self-imposed worship, their false humility and their harsh treatment of the body, but they lack any value in restraining sensual indulgence" (Colossians 2:20-21, 23, NIV). In other words, self-discipline can't really keep the flesh from sin.

That's because the flesh is so thoroughly imperfect. It can't *consistently* say "no" to sin. And even when the flesh looks pretty good on the outside, the inside is still a mess.

Check out these verses: "Every intent of the thoughts of [man's] heart was only evil continually" (Genesis 6:5). "All our righteous deeds are like a filthy garment" (Isaiah 64:6). "The heart is more deceitful than all else and is desperately sick" (Jeremiah 17:9). "For from within, out of men's hearts, come evil thoughts, sexual immorality, theft, murder, adultery, greed, malice, deceit, lewdness, envy, slander, arrogance, and folly. All these evils come from inside and make a man 'unclean'" (Mark 7:21-23, NIV). "The acts of the sinful nature are obvious: sexual immorality, impurity, and debauchery; idolatry and witchcraft; hatred, discord, jealousy, fits of rage, selfish ambition, dissensions, factions and envy, drunkenness, orgies and the like" (Galatians 5:19-21, NIV).

Gear-Up Saints?

Get the picture? People are not equipped to live God's style of behavior in their own strength. And unfortunately, even believers can live in the flesh, giving in to the old self instead of the new. Believers can be part of the Carnal Christian Club (1 Corinthians 3:1), a humanly moral group which tries to live a do-it-yourself Christian morality.

It's no good for an unbeliever or a carnal Christian to try to live God's supernatural system of right and wrong. No matter how self-disciplined, a person living in his own strength "cannot please

God" (Romans 8:5-8). "A man is not justified by observing the law" (Galatians 2:16, NIV). So God calls the actions of this Gear-Up approach, "dead works" (Hebrews 6:1). Gearing up old-self discipline to suppress the flesh's tendency to sin is like trying to pick yourself up by your own bootstraps. It's a dumb game.

Gearing up is also hypocritical. Somebody who tries to live morally in his own flesh power can't change himself to be really good (Jeremiah 13:23), but he's supposed to *act* as if he's good. He really can't stop sinning (Romans 7:15), but he's got to appear pious. He's a slave to sin (John 8:34; Colossians 1:13), but claims to be under God's control. The Gear-Up approach automatically breeds hypocrisy.

When my brother Tom was about eight, he proudly announced one night that he and some buddies had formed a club called the Temptations. "Don't panic, Mother," I said as she turned pale. "They're probably going to set up lemonade stands and take home lost cats. Stuff like that." Then a couple of days later, the police called to say that Tom and his little gang had been caught trying to break into a church. No charges would be filed.

"Why didn't you at least try for a bank, turkey?" I said as I got him in the car. It was two days before I convinced Tommy that the best thing to do to clear the situation was to go to the minister of the church and apologize. I drove him to the church office past a sign that said, "A Haven to All in the Name of the Lord," and bravely said I'd wait in the car.

Tommy trudged up the steps and I nodded to

myself about how good he'd feel to be forgiven. Five minutes passed. Ten minutes. Finally, Tommy came stumbling out of the office door, crying. He plopped into the seat next to me. "Well?" I tried to smile.

"He wouldn't forgive me," Tom said sobbing.

"You're kidding."

"He spent 15 minutes shouting at the top of his voice that I had scared him, that all his schedule was messed up now, that the police didn't do their job, that I'm headed for a life of crime, and that if I ever come near here again, he'll call the police."

I groaned. "That's great."

I'm sure Tom remembers the incident because of the pain, but I remember it mostly because it was all I could do not to get out of the car and kick that sign over. I was sick at the hypocrisy, of someone announcing he lived God's morality while apparently still practicing a Gear-Up morality.

Gearing up is frustrating. The Apostle Paul knew the agony of trying to master God's morality under his own steam: "I do not understand what I do. For what I want to do I do not do, but what I hate I do. . . . I have the desire to do what is good, but I cannot carry it out. For what I do is not the good that I want to do; no, the evil that I do not want to do—this I keep on doing. Now if I do what I do not want to do, it is no longer I who do it, but it is sin living in me that does it" (Romans 7:15, 18-20, NIV).

Got that? His old self couldn't fight the good fight. And neither can yours. You can't live right by gearing up your human self-discipline. It's a futile, hypocritical, frustrating hassle. Why bother?

The *Give-In* Approach

Fortunately for us, God doesn't expect our old selves to be good! He recognizes that the only way we can live up to His standards of morality is to give in to His control. Can God live righteously? Can God live righteously *in you?* Yep. The question is, will you give in to God's control?

Remember the old self/new self basics of discipleship (chapter 5)? Every Christian was made a new creation when he was born again (2 Corinthians 5:17). He's something special because he now has a new nature (2 Peter 1:4). And that new nature is designed to live righteously (Ephesians 4:24). God-in-us, the Holy Spirit, wants to control us "in order that the righteous requirements of the Law might be fully met in us, who do not live according to our sinful nature but according to the Spirit" (Romans 8:4, NIV).

See that? The requirements of God's morality are not fulfilled *by* us, they're fulfilled *in* us! God, in us, will live out His moral standards through our bodies. If we let Him. If we give in to Him. We've constantly got the choice.

"Do not offer the parts of your body to sin, as instruments of wickedness, but rather offer yourselves to God . . . and offer the parts of your body to Him as instruments of righteousness" (Romans 6:13, NIV). One of the words translated as "offer" in this verse means literally to "put at the service of." The word *instruments* means "tools, weapons of war." So make the choice. Don't bother putting yourself at the service of sin to be used as a tool of wickedness. Instead, let God use your body as His weapon for right living. Give in to Him.

The first time I rode a dirt bike, I didn't know beans about the bike or the course. I went flying off in all directions, throttling when I shouldn't have, braking when I shouldn't have, finally accelerating into an orange tree. I've still got the scar. That ride was like approaching life by *giving up* on moral principles, like pretending there are no rules. The rider is destined to smash into something. And to get hurt.

The next time I got out in the dirt I wised up a little. I decided it would be a better ride if somebody who knew the course and knew dirt bikes would climb on behind me and point out problem areas as I drove the machine. Unfortunately, I was on a bigger bike this time and wasn't yet skilled at changing gears, braking smoothly, etc. So on a short jaunt around the course, I succeeded in dumping both of us into two mudholes, a stream, and one barbed-wire fence. I was like the "moral" person who tries to tackle his unknown course of life with principles he hasn't mastered. I was like the "good" unbeliever in the world system, like the Christian who gears up fleshly self-discipline.

The third time out I met a dirt bike master. I let him control the machine. We had a good ride. So that's it. Give in to the control of the Master within you, and He'll help you live a moral lifestyle that makes sense.

10
The Disciple and *Religion in the* World

Max wheeled the forklift down the center aisle of the food warehouse. Suddenly, a blade on the front of the lift hooked on a corner support. Max screamed in Spanish as 4,000 boxes of Fruit Loops tumbled down. As a rookie warehouse worker, I was drafted to dig Max out and help him restack the cereal.

"I just got back from the hospital," he mumbled. "I guess I need more practice on the forklift."

I'd heard about the weird circumstances behind Max's hospital stay. "Why'd you do those things, Max?" I asked.

"The voice of God."

We stacked Fruit Loops as he told me the story. Max had come from Mexico to find work. He'd found work and he'd also found a new religion.

"The Messenger tells us what God wants, then we do the things God's voice says, *verdad*? I wanted to please God, so when I got home I put my finger in the battery acid—" Max held up his scarred finger. "And painted the crosses on my eyes. See?" He closed the lids to show off the crossed acid tracks on his eyelids. "I try to please God." He nodded. "Religion is good."

Max reminded me of the girl in Phoenix who asked for prayer for a friend. I was jotting down prayer requests at a Bible study.

"What's your friend's problem?"

"She's only a sophomore and she's pregnant."

"That's rough." I wrote the request.

"And when the baby's born she's going to sacrifice it."

I stopped writing. "What?"

"Satanism. She's going to sacrifice the baby. She says it's her religion."

Irritating Truth

As a disciple of Jesus, you *will* run into other "religious" disciples. With some 587 million Moslems, 475 million Hindus, 254 million Buddhists,

186 million Confucianists, and any number of off-the-wall cult fans in the world, you're bound to cross paths with members of world-system religions. And if you're living a serious style of Christian discipleship, expect some confrontation with these people.

Why? If Jesus had just claimed to be a man with some new ideas about God, Christian discipleship wouldn't threaten other religious systems. But that's not what He claimed. He said things like, "I am the Way, and the Truth, and the Life; no one comes to the Father but through Me" (John 14:6). And the Apostle Paul wrote of Jesus, "There is salvation in no one else; for there is no other name under heaven that has been given among men, by which we must be saved" (Acts 4:12). If you believe those Scriptures, and live like you believe them, be prepared to take flak from the two basic brands of world-system religions: the *works* brand and the *mystical* brand.

Working to Death

One super-scorching afternoon in Salt Lake City, Utah, I was going house to house, sharing the Gospel with whoever would listen. I learned fast to keep my nose out-of-range of slamming doors. And I was getting sweaty and discouraged when I came upon an old man mowing his lawn. He was Mr. Niceguy as long as we chatted about the weather, the lawn, his dog. But when I began sharing the Good News, his ears spurted steam. *Recipe for instant hostility*, I thought to myself, *just add the Gospel*.

I read to him without comment four passages of Scripture: "Believe in the Lord Jesus, and you shall be saved" (Acts 16:31). "If you confess with your mouth Jesus as Lord, and believe in your heart that God raised Him from the dead, you shall be saved" (Romans 10:9). "For by grace you have been saved through faith; and that not of yourselves, it is the gift of God; not as a result of works, that no one should boast" (Ephesians 2:8-9). "He saved us, not on the basis of deeds which we have done in righteousness, but according to His mercy" (Titus 3:5).

As soon as I finished reading the Titus verse, the man exploded so loudly that the whole neighborhood could hear. "You mean to say I can go out and murder somebody? I can go steal from my neighbor? I don't have to do anything to go to heaven? I can just live like the devil? Eh? Is that what you're saying, punk?"

"No, I was just reading the verses, sir."

He suddenly realized I was standing on his property and our little sharing time came to a close. But it reminded me of something I've realized time and time again as a Christian disciple: We live in a world where the make-your-self-perfect-by-works religions are strong and often hostile.

From bizarre cults to respectable, churchy set-ups, works-system religions typically say: "Be good. Meet our standards of conduct. Do the right things; don't do the wrong things." These groups fit nicely into Paul's evaluation: "For I bear them witness that they have a zeal for God, but not in accordance with knowledge. For not knowing about God's righteousness, and seeking to estab-lish their own, they did not subject themselves to the righteousness of God" (Romans 10:2-3). The goal of works-system religions is supposedly achieved by *doing*, by *working* at external standards of self-righteousness.

Most work-at-it religions are based on the idea that man is basically imperfect, that he has a sinful nature. So a drastic change is necessary, from imperfection to perfection, in order to be in right relationship with God. But does doing the right thing and not doing the wrong thing produce perfection? If a person chants the right phrases 15 times or gives the proper amount of money or any of the other "right things," does he suddenly wake up one morning to discover: "Yahoo! I'm perfect! Now God will accept me"?

Most people who are working their heads off in a works-system religion have some kind of spiritual scale in mind. They're working at piling up enough good things on one side of the scale to outweigh the bad things on the other side. If the good outweighs the bad, they think they're in!

The problem is, no amount of working and trying and balancing can change an imperfect nature into a perfect one. It's impossible for anyone to pull himself up to perfection by his religious bootstraps. No matter how hard people grunt and groan and work at it, the works system doesn't work!

The Magical Mystic Tour

There's another class of disciples loose in the world. These are the followers of various mystical religions. These religions generally stay away from a list of external do's and don'ts as a means of pleasing God. Instead, they teach that in a very abstract, out-of-this-world way, man is basically good. This goodness lies within him. And this goodness is essentially what other religions would label "God." More mystical terms would include the "Life Force," "Cosmic Consciousness," the "God-in-all-of-us," the "Cosmic Force of the Universe." The idea is that since this "God" with whom we want to merge is within us, we've just got to find Him—or to experience It.

Mystics seek this experience in a variety of ways—from chanting or meditating on mystical jive, to getting high on mushrooms or reds. Sometimes they even toss in some works-system tactics. They try to get rid of their imperfection through self-denial (starving themselves or living in a cave, for example). But the goal is basically the same. The mystic hopes to peel away layer after layer of his own identity in order to discover the "God" inside himself. And the mystic hopes, at that point of discovering God, to lose himself in Him (or It)—to merge with the Cosmic Force.

I remember the conversation I had with a mystical disciple on a Southern California college campus. He was hopping on one foot after the other, shaking a stick with jingle bells on it. His eyes were closed—possibly for effect, concentration, or to keep his ponytail-topknot from flicking his eyes.

"So the goal is to completely lose yourself in God?" I asked.

"Call it God if you like."

"But that's the goal?"

"You said it well, brother-man."

"Oh," I cleared my throat, stalling for time to

think. "Has anyone ever done this? Merged with God?"

"Yes, the fathers have done this. And some now may grow to this, like the quiet snuffing of a candle flame."

"Oh." I tried to remember why I was asking what I was asking. "How do you know they—they arrived? That they actually lost themselves in the Life Force?"

"So they have taught us. Through the centuries."

"Who taught you?"

"The fathers, brother-man."

"I thought they had merged with God?"

"It is so."

"You mean after they lost their consciousness, their selves, in God, they stepped back *into* themselves to tell you about it? I thought that once they'd merged, they were dissolved in God. But then how could they come back into themselves to tell you how it was?"

"Well, maybe the fathers had *almost* reached it when they told us the way."

"Well, then they wouldn't have known if it really worked or not. They wouldn't know if mystical searching was the way or not. They never experienced the merge if they were able to talk about it. Right?"

He stopped hopping. "Hey, look, buster, I'm trying to concentrate. Do you mind?" And off he hopped.

Do you catch the impossibility of the mystical approach to getting it together with God? It's impossible for a human being to lose his *self*, his identity. He will always be human. He will always be a person.

If a human being lost his human-beingness, he'd have no "self" left to teach, to communicate, to describe the path he'd taken to perfection. If he still communicated through his human consciousness, he couldn't be sure if he were on the right way to The Ultimate or not, since he wouldn't have arrived. (Getting dizzy?)

The fact is, the mystical road of inner experience is not the way to God. Sinful man—separated from God, "alienated from the life of God" (Ephesians 4:18, KJV),—can't find God inside himself.

Confronting the Counterfeits

Did you notice that both versions of world-system religion have tidbits of truth in them? Living God's lifestyle *does* have something to do with external conduct. The works-system gang is right on that point. And the mystics have the right idea in teaching that man's experience with God involves the inner, spiritual dimension of life. But just because I've got two ears and I can grunt doesn't make me a razorback hog. Just because most world-system religions preach tidbits of truth doesn't mean they're true ways to God.

A world-religion believer may be incredibly sincere. He may seem to have shreds of truth in his doctrine. He may be a nice guy. But he's still one of the horde that's cruising through the wide gate ("Be open-minded," these people say) and along the broad road ("All religions are OK," they say). And that road leads to destruction (Matthew 7:13).

The Viper Brood

Listen to what Jesus said to the *works* fans of His time: "Not everyone who says to Me, 'Lord, Lord,' will enter the kingdom of heaven. ... Many will say to Me on that day, 'Lord, Lord, did we not prophesy in Your name, and in Your name drive out demons and perform many miracles?' Then I will tell them plainly, 'I never knew you. Away from Me, you evildoers!' " (Matthew 7:21-23, NIV) Jesus said human do-gooders who haven't trusted in Him for salvation are "evildoers"!

Jesus told the ultra-religious, hard-working Pharisees: "I speak the things which I have seen with My Father; therefore you also do the things which you heard from *your* father. ... You are of your father the devil, and you want to do the desires of your father" (John 8:38, 44). He called them hypocrites; blind guides; white-washed tombs that are beautiful on the outside but are full of death inside; serpents; a brood of vipers (Matthew 23:23-33). You'd think people would catch on. God isn't fond of religion-by-works.

Mistaken Mystics

The Bible is just as negative on the mystical religions. The mystics, remember, think God can be found by looking inside yourself. But the Bible indicates that looking within will only reveal a heart that is "more deceitful than all else and desperately sick" (Jeremiah 17:9).

As to the mystic-system idea that self-denial

(without faith in Christ) can lead a person to God, Paul declares: "Let no one keep defrauding you of your prize by delighting in self-abasement. ... These are matters which have, to be sure, the appearance of wisdom in self-made religion and self-abasement and severe treatment of the body, but are of no value against fleshly indulgence" (Colossians 2:18, 23).

If God is so unimpressed with *works* and *mystical* religions, why can't their followers see that they're not on the narrow path "that leads to life"? (Matthew 7:14) The reason is that "the god of this world has blinded the minds of the unbelieving, that they might not see the light of the Gospel of the glory of Christ" (2 Corinthians 4:4). Satan, godfather of the world system, has pulled off a counterfeiting job to deceive his religious disciples (2 Corinthians 11:13-15).

Responding

What should be the disciple's response to people caught up in world-system religions?

Love 'em. Sometimes believers get so emotional in their defense of the Christian faith that they reject the world-religion *person* as well as his creed. But we're commanded to *love*—to love even our enemies (Matthew 5:44).

Bill Mullins and I wandered into a huge stadium one night where the Latter Day Saints—the Mormons—were celebrating a national youth convention. Bill and I had just completed some intensive training in the history and the false teachings of Mormonism. We couldn't wait to confront somebody.

I buttonholed a likely victim and asked, "If the *Book of Mormon* was translated into English in the 1820s, how come it's written in Elizabethan English just like the 1611 *King James Version* of the Bible?"

"Well," the kid began his memorized rebuttal.

"Here," I pulled out my well-studied *Book of Mormon*. "I can show you half a chapter in the *Book of Mormon* that's identical to the *King James Version* of Isaiah, even though—"

"Missionaries!" he began yelling. "I need a missionary!" Three Mormons leaped to the rescue.

Then Mullins and I waded in, slashing their beliefs with carefully sharpened arguments. The Mormons counterattacked, retreated, regrouped, and attacked again. Bill and I felt like the Two Musketeers dueling madly now with the dozen or so hostile enemies who had gathered.

Finally, Mullins made a point that nobody could argue against. We should have been jubilant in our victory. Instead, Bill and I looked at each other and realized what we'd been doing. We'd been arguing on a purely human level just to win the argument. We gulped, nodded at each other, and began backtracking toward the first principle of responding to people trapped in world-system religion: *Love* them first.

Jot it down in your world-view notebook: Even false disciples need love.

Confront 'em. But loving a person who's wrapped up in world-system religion doesn't mean you nod passively at his false beliefs. Loving in deed and *in truth* (1 John 3:18) means that false beliefs should be exposed. The Apostle Peter suggests that believers should always be ready to defend their beliefs to everyone who asks why Christ gives them hope (1 Peter 3:15). Jude urges disciples to "contend earnestly for the faith" (Jude 3).

People trapped in works and mysticism need out. They're drowning, and all world-system religion offers is a sinking raft. Be prepared with Bible knowledge to toss them the life preserver of the Good News.

Win 'em. Go ahead. Reject the false religions of the world. But think of world-religion people as individuals whom Christ died for. Realize that the reason they're "religious" at all is because, like every other person, they have a built-in need for a relationship with God. Remember that, as Jesus' disciples, we have the message that can meet that need:

"When someone becomes a Christian he becomes a brand-new person inside. He is not the same anymore. A new life has begun! All these new things are from God who brought us back to Himself through what Christ Jesus did. And God has given us the privilege of urging everyone to come into His favor and be reconciled to Him. For God was in Christ, restoring the world to Himself, no longer counting men's sins against them but blotting them out. This is the wonderful message He has given us to tell others" (2 Corinthians 5:17-19, LB).

11
The Disciple and the World in the Church

Do you realize that, if Jesus doesn't pull us all off the earth before then, you'll be part of the church of the next millennium—which begins in the year 2000? Think about it. How old will you be in the year 2010? What will your local church be like in 2020?

Most of the U.S. and Canadian populations will be over 60 years of age. More than 25 nations will have nuclear weapons. If current economic trends continue, money for paying church staff and for maintaining church properties will be scarce. In such an environment, what kind of church will you help develop? And how will you and your fellow disciples cope with the problem that's so easy to criticize in today's church: the problem of *worldliness in the church*?

Some people are as confused about what "the church" is as they are about pronouncing Chargoggagoggmanchauggauggagoggchaubunagungungamau, the name of a little lake in Webster, Massachusetts. So let's keep the definition simple: "Church" (*ekklesia* in the original Greek) means the "called-out ones." Every disciple—every real Christian—belongs to the church that belongs to Jesus Christ.

When clumps of disciples get together in places such as a house in Arica, Chile or an auditorium in Greenwich Village, we usually call these clumps *local churches*. The real church (all true believers) differs from local churches in size and in the fact that fake Christians are sometimes members of local churches. In the same way that weeds can grow undetected alongside genuine wheat, local churches can be infiltrated by false disciples (Matthew 13:24-30). But the real church of "called-out ones" is made up of all genuine believers in Jesus Christ.

The fact remains, not only is the local church made up of imperfect disciples, but it's also attended by some human "weeds." So expect problems in the local church. One of the hassles of discipleship is enjoying growth in the local church in spite of some choking thorns and thistles, in spite of the world system oozing through the brass-handled doors and stained-glass windows.

Even Pagans Love Christmas

The Bible mentions a local church that illustrates the problems of the world system in the church (Revelation 2:12-17). This particular church got together in a town called Pergamum, a wealthy city in what's now northwestern Turkey. Pergamum had a huge university and was a center of pagan religions. Athena, Dionysus, and Zeus topped the list of the city's "Top 100" gods.

When Christians brought the message of Christ to this city, Pergamumians decided Christianity would make a nice addition to their assortment of religions. So the local pagans started tossing in a few prayers to Jesus along with their worship of Dionysus and Zeus.

Sadly, a lot of the local Christians started mixing the pagan religions with their worship of Jesus. The world-system crowd got churchy and the church group got worldly.

This problem of the world in the church became an epidemic around the year A.D. 313. Constantine, emperor of the Roman Empire, was in a battle when he supposedly saw a vision of a cross in the sky. He took it as a good omen, and decided that by the sign of the cross he would be victorious. So he declared himself a Christian.

Whether he really became a believer or not is a toss-up. Anyway, because Constantine the new Christian was also the old emperor, everybody else suddenly became "Christians" too. Constantine made a law something like "You *will* be Christians and you *will* love it." Instant Christianity became the rage.

But the law brought some problems too: "What do we do next December during the winter solstice when we always used to cruise and carouse and have a holiday in honor of the nature gods?"

"No problem," said Constantine. "We'll just *pretend* that that's when Christ was born."

So the civilized world became "Christian" and the "Christian" church became worldly. It was as if Satan's system decided: "If you can't beat 'em, *join* 'em!" What happened—and what happens— when the world system infiltrates the church? Two big problems: Balaamism and Nicolaitanism. Let me explain.

The Teaching of Balaam

In case you didn't look up Revelation 2:12-17 (about Pergamum), here are verses 14 and 15: "I have a few things against you, because you have there some who hold the teaching of Balaam, who kept teaching Balak to put a stumbling block before the sons of Israel, to eat things sacrificed to idols, and to commit acts of immorality. Thus you also have some who in the same way hold the teaching of the Nicolaitans."

Read Balaam's story in Numbers 22—24. You'll see that Balaam's problem was that he tried to have the best of both worlds. He tried to be God's prophet and a heathen king's hit man at the same time.

Balak, king of Moab, was afraid of the Israelites

who had come into his land from Egypt. So, through bribery, he persuaded Balaam to put a curse on them. But when Balaam tried to give the curse, God stuck a blessing into his mouth. Instead of cursing, Balaam ended up blessing Israel. This happened three times.

You'd think Balaam would have gotten the message. But since he couldn't curse Israel, Balaam tried a new tactic. And this tactic is the essence of "the teaching of Balaam" (Revelation 2:14): He told Balak to corrupt Israel by inviting them to join in the immoral feasts of the god Baal-Peor (Numbers 31:16).

Balaamism is mixing the lust of the flesh, the lust of the eyes, and the pride of life with Christian worship and fellowship.

Is Balaamism a problem in the church today? Eh? I'll never forget the kid who ran up and down the aisles in the Hollywood Bowl during a Jesus-music concert. He'd find the best-looking girls and maul them with passionate hugs, yelling, "Oh, God bless this fellowship!" *Balaamism is the lust of the flesh in the church.*

Ego is another factor in the goings-on of many churches. The soloist steps all over the name of Christ in "real life," but the church has her sing regularly because her voice impresses the visitors. The new youth pastor is chosen on the basis of his looks, athletic ability, his fun stories, his enthusiasm—just like in the world system. The high schooler campaigns like a trooper for election to a youth group position, gets elected by a popularity vote, then never shows up for anything. *Balaamism is the "look-at-me" lust of the eyes in the church.*

"We don't worry about the picky little things in the Bible. I mean, a lot of those things just aren't practical in a church today. We have policies and forms of worship that we're comfortable with. And we'll stick with them, even if they don't fit the teachings of the New Testament." This message is echoed in too many local churches: "We'll be our own gods in our group decisions. We'll make up our own forms of Christianity." *The pride of life is alive and well—even in the local church.*

The teaching of Balaam. Watch out for it in your own attitudes in the church.

The People, No

A second problem that pops up when the world system oozes into the church is the "teaching of the Nicolaitans" (Revelation 2:15).

Though we don't know much historically about this group, we can get an idea of their beliefs from their name. It comes from *nikao*, "to conquer," and *loas*, "the people." Nicolaitan teaching held that God's people needed to be ruled over by a separate class, just as the common people "needed" to be ruled by the aristocrats. The Nicolaitans believed that this group would be spiritually *above* the people, the *laos*. The equal brotherhood of disciples (Matthew 23:8) would be sliced up into two categories of believers: the "ruling class" and the "commoners." Christ's command that church leaders be servants—not lords (Matthew 20:25)—would be ignored.

The clergy would tell the people what God said in His Word. They would perform religious rituals with the people as spectators. Eventually, this "upper class" of Christians would actually forgive sins and damn people to hell if they wanted to.

What's the big attraction to the Nicolaitan teaching? *None!* you're probably thinking. But there must be some attraction, because Nicolaitan attitudes are alive and well in many churches today. Maybe Nicolaitanism is appealing because it relieves people of responsibility. People don't have to pray and read the Bible in order to know God's will for them. They don't have to actively participate in worship. They can just leave everything to the preacher, or the youth group leader.

I tried an experiment in breaking the Nicolaitan habit in a Sunday School class. First I told Shelly and Tammy to watch what was about to happen. Then I announced, "All right. You've got four minutes as a group to decide how to use the $50 I'm going to donate to the class." Everybody just sat there yawning, wondering what was going on. Mike looked at Mitch, Mitch shrugged to Allison. "Three minutes," I said.

"I think he means it," said Kendall. "What'll we do?" Everybody stared at each other for another minute and a half.

"Whatever." Mike yawned.

"One minute," I said.

Marty and Rodney mumbled something about pizza. Nathan shrugged. Finally Kendall said, "A party. We can have it at my house. Get pizza and stuff. . . ."

"Time!" I announced. "OK, as a group, what did you decide?"

"Have a party at Kendall's," mumbled Randy.

"Is everybody in agreement?" Most of them

yawned and nodded absently. "What happened here, Shelly?" I asked.

"Well, everybody didn't quite believe you at first. They all kind of sat back waiting to see what would happen. Finally, Kendall gave the idea for a party at his house."

"Do you think that's what the other people in the room really felt should be done with the $50?"

"Probably not everybody."

"But the entire class let Kendall decide for them, right?" Shelly nodded and Kendall slouched in his chair, embarrassed. I asked Tammy, "Why?"

"Probably," she said, "because that way, if the party bombed, they could blame Kendall. They could feel they weren't responsible for the use of the money. So they just kept quiet till somebody stuck his neck out."

I think the following quotes are terrific examples of the way people won't take responsibility for their own actions. These statements are taken from actual insurance company files, from policyholders' reports on why they were involved in traffic accidents:

"My car was legally parked as it backed into the other vehicle."

"I pulled away from the side of the road, glanced at my mother-in-law, and headed over the embankment."

"The telephone pole was approaching. I was attempting to swerve out of its way when it struck my front end."

"The cause of this accident was a little guy in a small car with a big mouth."

"An invisible car came out of nowhere, struck my vehicle, and vanished."

Invisible cars, walking telephone poles—people come up with some creative ways of getting out of responsibility. And that's the main reason the teaching of the Nicolaitans is still around today.

Here are some questions that could help detect any Nicolaitan attitudes you might have:

- Do you feel that your pastor or youth pastor is responsible for your spiritual growth?
- Do you feel that the pastor of your church can always interpret the Bible better than anyone else in the congregation?
- Do you think of positions of leadership in the church as executive roles or as servant roles? Why?
- Are the "successful" people of your church—the wealthy and the popular—usually your choice candidates for leadership positions?

The Pergamum Purge

Ready for a quick review? When the world system oozes into the church, at least two problems often occur (they're the same problems that surfaced in the Pergamum church): *Balaamism*, remember, is the problem of mixing the lust of the flesh, the lust of the eyes, and the pride of life with Christian worship and fellowship. *Nicolaitanism* is the problem of placing responsibility for encouraging spiritual growth and finding God's will into the hands of an elite group.

Now, what do you do if, with Spirit-guided discernment, you glimpse these problems in you or in your church?

First, clean out your head and protect your ears from false teaching, the kind that mixes world-system philosophies with biblical Christianity (Galatians 1:8; Romans 16:17-18; 2 John 7-11; Jude).

Second, don't form a Purge-the-Pergamums Vigilante Committee. You won't accomplish much by going on a local-church witch-hunt for Balaams and Nicolaitans. Forget about crusades to clean out the church; the Lord of the harvest will take care of the weeds (Matthew 13:24-30). Concentrate instead on denying your old self, living in your new self, and following Christ.

Abide in His Word. "If you abide in My Word, then you are truly disciples of Mine" (John 8:31). The Bible will give you the kind of insight you need to discern whether your church-related attitudes are biblical or Pergamumian.

Practice love. "By this will all men know that you are My disciples, if you have love for one another" (John 13:35). Loving each other in the church by fulfilling God's commands toward one another (2 John 6) is vital. Without this a church or youth group usually divides into little cliques of "holier-than-thous," "the worldly gang," and "middle-of-the-roaders." And that brings on Pergamumianism at its ugliest.

Bear fruit. "By this is My Father glorified, that you bear much fruit, and so prove to be My disciples" (John 15:8). The "fruit" of discipleship is partially defined in John 4:36 as the people whom a disciple leads to Christ. But the idea of spiritual fruit is expanded in Galatians 5:22-23 to include spiritual growth: "The fruit of the Spirit is love, joy, peace, patience, kindness, goodness, faithfulness, gentleness, self-control."

Be aware of the Pergamum problem, especially in your own attitudes. But instead of huffing and puffing about all the imperfections in the church, get on with the business of discipleship!

So much for the world in the church. Now let's tackle a more positive subject: the church in the world.

12
The Disciple and the Church in the World

Dusk. Four soldiers sit around a table on the second floor of a bombed-out building. Rockets whistle overhead and someone screams in the street below.

The soldier with the cleanest uniform complains, "I still say tacos are too messy. If we're going to have a decent dinner, the menu shouldn't include tacos. The sauce drips out. The lettuce falls on your lap—"

A grenade explodes in the basement of the building, shaking the table where the four soldiers sit. "I'll bet that one got old Jeep downstairs," says a second soldier. "Boy, did he get hit with some shrapnel last month! Did you guys hear about it? Huh? How about you, Joey? Did you hear?"

"Yeah," says Joey, grinning. "I hear it was real bad."

The soldier begins his gory tale, drowning out old Jeep's moan from downstairs.

"Enough gossip," interrupts the fourth man. "I'm sick of it!" He flicks a cigarette across the room. "And I'm sick of the Army. I'd like to find a good hideout somewhere and sit out the rest of this war. Maybe I'll apply for a discharge."

A soldier with a different colored uniform slinks unnoticed up the dark stairway.

"Let's get back to the tacos," snaps the first soldier, "although I must say I think you're right about this war. I mean, we've never even seen the Commander. So it's difficult to trust Him, you know? Sometimes I wonder if the enemy is really as hostile as the Commander says."

From the shadows of the doorway, metal flashes. Joey grunts in disbelief and falls moaning to the floor, a dagger lodged between his shoulder blades. The enemy commando dives back down the stairs.

"Wonder how they're doing at the front?" asks the second soldier, trying not to notice Joey.

"The front? I wonder where it is?" mutters the soldier with the clean uniform. "It's been a long time since I looked at the Commander's battle plans."

A 60mm shell whines overhead and explodes in the next building. Screams and frantic calls for help follow the sound of the blast.

"Definitely not—" The first soldier drums his fingers on the table. "Definitely not tacos for dinner."

Like these four ineffective soldiers, a church that pretends it's not battling the world system is living a lie. It's wasting its time worrying about nonessentials. But you know by now that you and your church aren't cloistered in a demilitarized zone. You know, since it faces an Enemy who's determined to destroy mankind, that the purpose of the church is not to plan menus. So let's look at it: the purpose of the church in the world.

Battle Plan

You probably know the verses. They're usually called *The Great Commission*: "Go therefore and make disciples of all the nations, baptizing them in the name of the Father and the Son and the Holy Spirit, teaching them to observe all that I commanded you; and lo, I am with you always, even to the end of the age" (Matthew 28:19-20).

These are our Commander's instructions. So, as soldiers of His army, the church, we need to make sure we understand the plan. Let's take a closer look at the church's marching orders.

Where. Jesus' command is to "go." And ultimately this part of His plan for the church includes going to the whole world (Mark 16:15). But, wherever the Lord leads an individual disciple to *go*, the important thing for him is to get involved in the plan.

For some of the original disciples who heard Jesus' command with their own ears, "go therefore" meant going to other countries to share the Gospel. For others it meant going back to their homes in Jerusalem and getting involved in Christ's plan. For today's disciples, the command to "go" might mean going overseas. But it might just as well mean getting involved for Christ while *going* to work, to Grandma's, to school, or to Leroy's Southern-Fried Artichoke Stand.

The point is, don't wait around for a call to Bunga-bunga Land. The Lord knows you have opportunities right now to accomplish His purpose for your life and for His church. *Going* to work, *going* to Wyoming for the summer, *going* on a date—make sure you're involved in doing what God designed you to do—which is?

What. God's design for the believer and for groups of believers is specific: "All authority in heaven and on earth is given to Me. Go therefore and *make disciples* of all nations" (Matthew 28:18-19, italics mine).

Here it is, folks. The church's purpose is to "make disciples." Disciples are to make more disciples. Their purpose is not to be a political party, or to be experts at sponsoring pancake sales. Their primary purpose is not to build the biggest auditoriums in town or to eat a lot of potluck dinners. The main purpose of the church is to make disciples. The main purpose of your life, as part of the church, is to make disciples—to make yourself a stronger, more mature disciple and to make others into Jesus' disciples. Write it down:

The Purpose of My Church and My Purpose as Part of That Church Is to Make Disciples.

How. "Baptizing them in the name of the Father and the Son and the Holy Spirit, teaching them to observe all that I commanded you" (Matthew 28:19-20).

The first step in becoming a disciple is receiving Christ—and through Him, salvation. Likewise, the first step in making disciples is leading people to receive Christ. And "baptizing," in this verse, implies just that—that a person has been led to the Lord and is giving evidence of his salvation through the outward sign of baptism.

I'll never forget the gawking onlookers at San Jose City College who watched a group of new Christians being baptized in the school pool. Friends, enemies, and curious passersby hung onto the chain link fence around the pool as one student after another shouted out that he'd made Jesus his Lord, and then was dunked at the four-foot mark.

For those new believers, as for every disciple, baptism proclaimed their salvation. Baptism announced their spiritual birth into God's family (John 3:7). But leading people to Christ is just the beginning of the disciple-making process.

A second phase of making disciples is "teaching them to observe all that I commanded you" (Matthew 28:20). The life of discipleship doesn't end where it started—at spiritual birth. Babies are born to grow. Spiritual growth comes from spiritual food

(1 Peter 2:2)—from learning and doing all that God has commanded.

When I was in college, a group of us Christians would gather near the cafeteria every Friday after lunch, with knots in our stomachs. (I'm sure the knots were related not so much to the cafeteria as to why we were meeting.) When the group was assembled, we'd figure out who was going to ride with whom and who would be whose "buddy." Then we'd drive from our college to a nearby community college, and spread out in groups of twos around the campus to conduct an evangelistic survey.

One day my buddy and I were surveying one student after another, asking at the conclusion of each questionnaire if we could share with them what Christ had done in our lives. Suddenly a hostile-looking young man came toward us. I'd been harassed before by such types, so I jumped to the offensive by asking, "Like to take a community survey?"

"I've been looking for you," he said sternly. "Who do you represent?"

I gulped. "We, uh, we don't really represent anybody."

You're Christians, right?"

"Yeah. Born-again believers."

"Will you sit down with me for a minute?" He pointed toward a bench, and my spirits rose. *He wants to hear how to receive Christ*, I figured. I could already envision the joy and abundant humility with which I would report this decision to the group.

But what the guy did was thoroughly blister my ears. As I studied the brickwork under the bench, he told me how the previous semester he'd been sitting on that very bench. I had approached him with the very same survey, he reminded me, and he had decided to follow Christ.

Not long after the decision, he'd had some serious problems, and needed to talk to another believer. But he couldn't find anyone. He said that I hadn't left my name or address or phone number with him, so he couldn't contact me. He'd changed classes, so he wasn't free when I usually came to the campus. Finally, he told me that he'd just given up. As we sat on that bench together, he looked me in the eye and said he didn't feel anything but bad and guilty whenever he thought about God anymore. And he said he wanted *out* of Christianity for good.

As I felt myself sliding slimily under the bench, I had a fleeting urge to try to defend myself. But there really wasn't much I could say.

Now, nobody with half a brain leaves a newborn baby sitting by himself on a bench out in the cold. That's true with spiritual as well as physical babies. Spiritual birth demands spiritual feeding and care. Our purpose as believers involves more than chalking up first-time decisions for Christ. Christ told His followers to *make disciples*. And since discipleship involves a believer's total lifestyle in the real world, making disciples is a long-haul process!

So there you have it, Christ's plan for building His kingdom and defeating the world system: disciples *reaching* and *training* others to be His disciples.

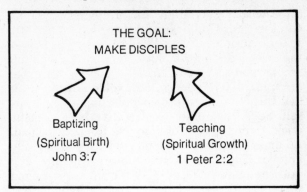

THE GOAL:
MAKE DISCIPLES

Baptizing
(Spiritual Birth)
John 3:7

Teaching
(Spiritual Growth)
1 Peter 2:2

Down to You

So far we've been talking in pretty theoretical terms, right? Let's get down to specifics. Let's get down to you.

It's 1:30 in the morning. I'm in the mountains by an ice-covered pond called Lake Return. The high schoolers on this weekend retreat are finally snoozing after a woolly game of "Super Spy" in the snow. It's windy with a clear sky full of stars, and the trees are cracking in the wind. It's a good time to talk.

I know something about you. I figure that if you've read this far, either you've been arm-twisted into doing it for a Sunday School or Bible study session, or you really want to live a Christian lifestyle in the world. Or maybe both. I know you want more than a humdrum life of religious meetings and "pie in the sky by and by." God wants more than that for you too. He wants some dazzle, some wisdom, some joy and strength for you as you live your God-designed life. So get this:

The reason you're on Planet Earth right now—the reason God didn't pluck you up to heaven the second you received Christ—is so you can make disciples. You're here to be involved in the spiritual birth and growth of people, including yourself. See? The reason you're alive isn't to make bucks or cut records or graduate from law school. All those things are incidental to what you're really here for. The shoemaker-missionary William Carey said something like this: "My business is saving souls; I just cobble shoes to make a living." (Not an exact quote there; exact quotes are hard to come by in the middle of winter nights at Lake Return.)

Get Dangerous

Well, the guys aren't asleep yet after all. They're showing off their wilderness skills by comparing birdcalls—which reminds me of my conversation with Tracy. When I talked to her about being involved in disciple-making, she said, "But I was witnessing to a couple of girls who said they didn't believe in God or heaven or hell and I just stood there and went 'duuhhh.' What do you say to people like that?"

"Is it your job to convince them," I replied, "to prove something to them? Or is your job just to be a witness who says, 'Hey, this is what happened to me, and that's the truth'? They can take it or leave it. You can't force somebody to be born again. Leave the results to God. But don't give up. Stay involved in disciple-making."

"How?" she said. "I don't like knocking on doors—that kind of evangelism."

"What do you like to do?" I asked.

Tracy looked surprised. "Well, I like hunting. Pheasant hunting."

"Great. Organize a hunting club. Then when you get outside for the hunt, look for opportunities to share Christ with whomever you're around."

"That's dumb," Tracy decided.

But I think Tracy was wrong. It's not such a dumb idea. It's different, maybe a little daring, but not dumb. Matter of fact, there are lots of not-dumb ideas you could use to reach people for Christ; for example:

• Produce a freebie radio show for your local station designed to reach non-Christians.

• Write your own tracts that explain real Christianity in terms that non-Christians can understand.

• Ask a friend if anybody has ever explained real Christianity to him.

• Become a street comic who can communicate Christ through humor.

• Get a music group together that can communicate to non-Christians.

• Write about Christ to kids from a pen-pals-wanted column.

• Form a club or just spontaneously witness to people who are interested in things you're interested in—joggers or truckers or hot-air balloonists or bikers or quilters or skiers or poets or mechanics.

• Knock on doors and share Christ with whoever answers.

• Design a bumper sticker with a Christian message to non-Christians; have it printed up and distribute the stickers to friends.

And so on and so on. It's getting later and I suddenly remember I have to crawl out of the sack for an early-morning Bible study. So I've got to cut the list off somewhere. The point is, that as a natural part of your lifestyle, you've got tons of opportunities to be involved in spiritual birth. You've got the power to do it (Acts 1:8), and you've got the special gifts you need to do it *in your own way* (1 Corinthians 12:7-11).

Get your brain out of the rut that says only "professional Christians" such as missionaries or evangelists are the ones who can really communicate Christ with others. And remember that the ways God will use you will be unique since you're a unique person. You might be criticized. ("Whoever heard of a ministry as a Christ-sharing scuba diver?") You might not fit into the traditions of *cultural Christian* evangelism. But your goal in life isn't to promote cultural Christianity, is it? Your goal is to make real disciples. So get dangerous for Christ. Let the Spirit use you in His program of bringing salvation to slaves of the world system.

Get Growing

At the same time, expect Him to use you in quiet or crazy or traditional ways to bring spiritual *growth* into the lives of His disciples as you:

• Start a Christian sports ministry or car club or scientific organization or service group.

• Write notes of encouragement to believers in your church.

• Learn how to lead people to Christ and then teach other disciples how to do it.

• Get together a small group of Christians for regular prayer sessions.

• Design and display posters/paintings/sculptures that motivate Christians.

• Disciple (teach and lead) a less mature Christian brother or sister.

• Grow by feeding on and acting on God's Word.

• Write books or poems or stories or articles or plays or movie scripts or songs for Christians.

• Adopt an elderly Christian whom you visit, read Scripture to, pray with, and run errands for.

• Meet regularly with other believers for Bible study.

• Sing songs that encourage and inspire other Christians.

• Lead a Bible study group for younger Christians.

• Type memory verse cards for people in your church to use.

• Produce a slide-tape presentation or film on the purpose of the church.

• Gather and deliver food and clothes for needy Christians.

• Visit or phone Christians who are sick or discouraged or who have quit having fellowship with the rest of the believers in your church.

• Sharpen your speaking skills and use them to equip other Christians for evangelism and growth.

• Produce art that makes Christians think.

• Help other believers in practical ways as they're involved in *their* part of the birth/growth process: You might volunteer as a church janitor, build a radio tower for Christian broadcasts, type correspondence for a church or Christian organization, fix the cars/planes/office equipment/generators/plumbing/electrical equipment for Christian groups, etc.

Again, the list is endless. God can use you to aid spiritual growth in ways that nobody on earth has ever dreamed! Somehow, in some ministry, you can fulfill your purpose as a believer: to make disciples through spiritual birth and growth.

All these ministries can go on while you're making your living as a garbageperson or mailperson or doctor or roughneck or housewife or corporate executive. The Apostle Paul made tents for a while to earn his living so he could teach and preach (Acts 18:1-4). Though by vocation you might be an astronaut or a chicken plucker, at heart you're a *minister* (2 Corinthians 5:18).

Maybe God designed you to enjoy a career in ice-cream tasting and a ministry in sharing Christ with the terminally ill. Don't ever think of yourself as a second-class disciple, as someone who isn't very spiritual, because you just taste ice cream during working hours. God needs ice-cream tasters who'll minister in the real world.

Then again, maybe God designed you to fit your career together with your ministry. You could be a *vocational minister*. That is, you could be one who earns a living by ministering. Maybe God wants you to have a writing career and to write about some aspect of discipleship. Maybe He wants you to be a psychologist and to counsel Christians. Maybe God will lead you into a career of flying to remote areas to promote spiritual birth and growth. "Full-time Christian service" isn't limited to being a pastor, a missionary, a youth minister, a Christian education specialist, or a church music director.

There are hundreds of ways for a disciple to be involved in disciple-making. And there's one way that's just right for you. But however you do it, get out there! Right in the thick of the world system.

You and your fellow disciples, the church, can be the "salt of the earth" (Matthew 5:13). You can help cure the rot of the world system, flavoring every situation you step into, making people thirsty for God. You can be the "light of the world" (Matthew 5:14). As light, you can expose darkness, bring warmth, let blind people see. As a church, you can make beautiful disciples together. You can beat the world system. You can overcome the world (1 John 5:4-5). And the gates of hell won't prevail against you (Matthew 16:18).